ROBINSON CRUSOE

ISLAND MYTHS AND THE NOVEL

Twayne's Masterwork Studies

Robert Lecker, General Editor

ROBINSON CRUSOE

ISLAND MYTHS AND THE NOVEL

Michael Seidel

Twayne Publishers * Boston
A Division of G. K. Hall & Co.

Robinson Crusoe: Island Myths and the Novel
Michael Seidel

Twayne's Masterwork Study, No. 64
Copyright 1991 by G. K. Hall & Co.
All rights reserved.
Published by Twayne Publishers
A division of G. K. Hall & Co.
70 Lincoln Street
Boston, Massachusetts 02111

Copyediting supervised by Barbara Sutton
Book production by Gabrielle B. McDonald
Typset in Sabon with Kennerly display type
by Evergreen Publishing Services, Inc. of Guilderland, NY.

The paper used in this publication meets the minimum requirements of American National Standard for Information Sciences—Permanence of Paper for Printed Library materials, ANSI Z39.48-1984. ⊚™

Printed and bound in the United States of America

Library of Congress Cataloging-in-Publication Data

Seidel, Michael, 1943—
      Robinson Crusoe : island myths and the novel / Michael Seidel.
         p.   cm. — (Twayne's masterwork studies)
      Includes bibliographical references and index.
      ISBN 0-8057-8074-2 (alk. paper). — ISBN 0-8057-8120-X (pbk. :
alk. paper)
      1. Defoe, Daniel, 1661?-1731. Robinson Crusoe. 2. Islands in
literature. I. Title. II. Series.
   PR3403.Z5S45   1991
   823'.5—dc20
                                                        90-43231
                                                            CIP

0-8057-8074-2 (alk. paper) 10 9 8 7 6 5 4 3 2 1
0-8057-8120-x (pbk. alk. paper) 10 9 8 7 6 5 4 3 2 1

Contents

Note on the References

I have cited the standard edition of *The Life and Strange Surprizing Adventures of Robinson Crusoe, of York, Mariner*, edited with an introduction by J. Donald Crowley (Oxford: Oxford University Press, 1972). This is part of the readily available Oxford English Novels series under the general editorship of James Kinsley. Crowley's text has several advantages: it is based on the first edition of *Crusoe;* its textual notes collate in an accessible manner the editions of the work published in Defoe's lifetime; and its explanatory notes are brief and sensible. Citations from *The Farther Adventures of Robinson Crusoe* (1719) and *Serious Reflections during the Life and Surprising Adventures of Robinson Crusoe* (1720) are taken from the multi-volume edition *The Works of Daniel Defoe*, edited by G. H. Maynadier (New York: Sproul, 1903–4).

The best handbook text of *Robinson Crusoe* is the Norton Critical Edition, edited by Michael Shinagel (New York: W. W. Norton, 1975), which contains valuable material from Defoe's sequel volumes of the *Crusoe* saga as well as other contemporary background material useful for understanding the contexts of the narrative. Shinagel also includes a historical range of critical reaction to *Crusoe* over the centuries and a number of key modern day essays that reflect major currents of thinking about Defoe's masterpiece.

Daniel Defoe
Von der Gucht engraving.

Chronology: Daniel Defoe's Life and Works

1659	[Robinson Crusoe begins his fictional twenty-eight-year reign as island castaway on 30 September.]
1660	Charles II is restored to English throne after twelve-year exile. Defoe is born ca. 30 September to James and Alice Foe in Cripplegate parish of London just outside the old city gates. Originally a tallow chandler, James Foe is by the time of Daniel's birth a jack of all economic trades, part accountant, part estate factor, part merchant.
1662	Charles II signs Act of Uniformity 12 May banning nonconformers from the Anglican Church. Defoe's Dissenting family joins the meeting house services of Dr. Samuel Annesley.
1663–1665	The first acts of the Clarendon Code, a series of measures restricting the civil and religious rights of Dissenters, are put into effect. Defoe's family is barred from worship within a five-mile radius of the city walls of London. Defoe would never forget the intolerance of these days; his anti-Stuart sentiment is bred in him early.
1665	Bubonic Plague ravages London. Defoe's family leaves town, but an uncle may have remained to run family warehouse business. Defoe re-creates this period brilliantly later in his *Journal of the Plague Year* (1722).
1666	Great Fire of London levels much of city.
1674–1679	Defoe attends the rigorous and scientifically minded Morton's Academy at Newington Green, the excellent Dissenting college run by Charles Morton, who would later play a leading role in the founding of Harvard University. Reads widely and well at Morton's and studies everything from the classics to modern history, geography, physical science, and, most prominently, natural law. One of his schoolmates is named Timothy Cruso, a later acquaintance in London as well. The moniker reappears with an "e" for Defoe's famous castaway.

1678–1681   The Popish Plot conspiracy to re-Catholicize England embroils the land. During the turmoil of this overblown but dangerous crisis, the two-party system forms in England under the guidance of the Earl of Shaftesbury, John Locke, and the Green Ribbon Club. At this time Defoe and fellow students at Morton's cultivate active and organized opposition to absolutist, divine right, dynastic policies promulgated by the Stuarts.

1679   Tours Europe, the first of many travels abroad.

1681   Abjures the call to serve in the Presbyterian ministry, which had been his early vocational plan, and, with his family's help, begins an increasingly successful importing and exporting business as a linen factor.

1683   Rye House Plot against the Crown ends in disaster as Charles II executes presumed conspirators. These are dark days for all who distrusted the Restoration regime, but Defoe continues to improve his business position in London.

1684   On 1 January marries Mary Tuffley, daughter of a wine cooper and possessor of a considerable dowry of £3700. Begins traveling extensively throughout England, in Scotland, and on the Continent to promote his business interests.

1685   Participates in the horse cavalry of the duke of Monmouth's forces during a brief rebellion against James II after the death of Charles II. Monmouth's defeat is ignominious in the bad weather at the Battle of Sedgemoor, and Defoe is fortunate not to be nabbed and tried for his marginal role by the notorious Bloody Assizes run by Lord Jeffreys. Three of Defoe's former Morton's Academy schoolmates lose their lives in this abortive revolt.

1685–1689   Involves himself in multiple trade and merchant ventures, including an interest in a passenger transport ship to the New World, the *Batchelor,* and a cargo ship named *Desire.*

1688   On 26 January becomes a member of his father's livery company, the Butchers', which, to his delight, was Shakespeare's livery company as well. Is wealthy enough to maintain a city and country home. William of Orange lands in England in November 1688, and the Glorious (or Bloodless) Revolution deposing James II is complete by December. Defoe, who writes political tracts against the policies of James II, ceremoniously rides to greet William's invading army.

1692   Overextends financially in the post-Revolution boom economy and faces lawsuits by several creditors seeking £17,000. Claims he incurred massive losses in marine insurance during William's foreign wars but also speculates in schemes to recover buried treasure and to corner the perfume-producing civet cat market of London. His declared bankruptcy subjects him to brief imprisonments in the Fleet and King's Bench prisons, and he thinks of his financial disaster as a shipwreck, a metaphor that would take literal shape in *Robinson Crusoe*.

1694   Is set back on his feet financially by influential friends in King William's government, including Charles Montagu, a minister, and Dalby Thomas, a wealthy merchant. Begins his brick- and tile-manufacturing venture at Tilbury, which produces a variety of tile manufactures in addition to pantiles for the construction of the Greenwich Hospital. [Crusoe's pride in fashioning a clay pipe on his island touches on these Tilbury manufactures.]

1695   Affixes the preface "De" to his name officially. Dalby Thomas appoints him accountant to the Glass Duty Commission. Thomas, among other interests, later controls the African slave trade monopoly and gives Defoe a £800 piece of the action. [Robinson Crusoe, for better or worse, sought an even larger piece of the slave trade before his shipwreck.]

1697   Treaty of Ryswick ends French war. Defoe publishes his first major prose work, *An Essay upon Projects*, filled with schemes and plans to reform England's economic, social, and educational life. He is at this time secretly serving King William's government as an advisor on internal and foreign affairs.

1698   Has a hand in framing parts of the Partition Treaties devised for the crumbling Spanish empire. Also directly offers a proposal to King William for settling key South American coastal territories, including the Orinoco River basin where *Robinson Crusoe* is set. This commercial trade and colonization project becomes one of the dreams of Defoe's life; he would launch it again in 1711 at the time of the South Sea Trade Company and yet again in 1719, the year he publishes *Crusoe*.

1701   Publishes his immensely popular poem, *The True-Born Englishman*, satirizing xenophobic opposition to his hero and patron, King William.

1702	William III dies; Queen Anne reigns. War of Spanish Succession begins. Defoe publishes his satiric tract, *The Shortest Way with the Dissenters,* a mimicry of schemes for selective execution and mass emigration of all religious undesirables in England. To his horror, the pamphlet is praised by leading officials of the established church, even though the government declares Defoe and his printer outlaws and hunts them for sedition.
1703	Fined, pilloried, and imprisoned for the *Shortest Way* hoax; is released from Newgate six months later by agreeing to spy for Tory government in Scotland in the employ of Robert Harley, one of Anne's leading ministers.
1704	The duke of Marlborough wins the Battle of Blenheim on the Continent. Alexander Selkirk, a partial model for Crusoe's adventure, is castaway on the isle of Juan Fernandez off Pacific coast of South America (opposite to Crusoe's coast), where he will remain for four years. Defoe begins his one-man periodical, the *Review,* published two and three times a week for nine years. He also writes a full-length book, *The Storm,* investigating the effects of a vicious gale in the British isles the year before. The combination of realistic detail and providential speculation that marks this book reappears as characteristic of Defoe's fiction two decades later.
1705	Writes *The Consolidator,* his first extended piece of prose fiction, a narrative allegory of contemporary history and politics portrayed on the moon.
1706	Writes his major political poem, a twelve-book opus in couplets, *Jure Divino,* against the notion of divine right tyranny in history and, primarily, against the Stuart kings.
1707	Act of Scottish Union complete. Defoe had been working in secret for the government in support of the union for years.
1708	Serves Anne's minister, Lord Treasurer Godolfin, after Defoe's patron, Robert Harley, was temporarily put out of office.
1709	Alexander Selkirk rescued by Woodes Rogers expedition after four years on the island of Juan Ferandez.
1711	Advises Harley, back in office, on formation of South Sea Company. Repeats his scheme to settle Orinoco River basin and other coastal areas of South America.
1712	Woodes Rogers's *Cruising Voyage* published with account of Alexander Selkirk's ordeal.

Chronology

1713	Treaty of Utrecht ends long War of Spanish Succession. Defoe arrested briefly again for mock-seditious Jacobite pamphlets before the Hanoverian Succession and the arrival of George I. Richard Steele writes popular account of Alexander Selkirk's adventure.
1714	Queen Anne dies; Robert Harley falls as minister; George I, first Hanoverian king, accedes to throne.
1715	Publishes *The Family Instructor*, composite of advice, fictional scenarios, and dialogues, which went through eight editions by 1720. Also writes and spies for the Whig ministry (and continues to do so for the rest of his life). Jacobite rebellion easily put down by Hanoverian regime.
1718	Renewed war with Spain; Defoe recommends conciliatory posture as he does implicitly in *Crusoe*. New edition of Woodes Rogers's *Cruising Voyage* keeps the famous Alexander Selkirk account very much in the public eye. Defoe writes for several Tory periodicals serving as journalistic mole for the Whig government.
1719	Publishes *Robinson Crusoe*, first and second parts. Again renews his schemes for South African coastal colony, mentioning Orinoco River basin, the location of Crusoe's island, as an appealing possibility.
1720	Publishes his *Serious Reflections on Robinson Crusoe, Captain Singleton*, and *Memoirs of a Cavalier*. South Sea Bubble bursts in England and in Europe, following wild speculation on stock of the South Sea Trading Company and ending any hope for Defoe's colonization schemes.
1721	Robert Walpole comes to power as lord treasurer. Defoe works for him as a propagandist and as journalistic mole on antigovernment periodicals.
1722	Publishes *Moll Flanders, Colonel Jack*, and *A Journal of the Plague Year*.
1724	Publishes *Roxana, A Tour Thro' the whole Island of Great Britain*, and *A General History of the Pyrates*.
1725	Publishes *The Complete English Tradesman*.
1726	Publishes *The History of the Devil*. Jonathan Swift publishes *Gulliver's Travels*, much of which parodies the success of *Robinson Crusoe* and attacks its premises.

1727	George I dies; George II accedes to throne. Defoe publishes *Conjugal Lewdness*, another conduct book.
1728	Publishes *A Plan of English Commerce*.
1731	Dies of "a lethargy" on 24 April in Ropemaker's Alley, pursued by creditors right to the end. He is buried in Bunhill Fields. James Sutherland's words on Defoe's death are eloquent and moving: "There have been few men in any generation so indomitably alive for seventy years as Daniel Defoe was alive, and who dying can make us feel so sharply the finality of death. When he breathed his last in the lodging-house in Ropemaker's Alley, a source of energy was suddenly cut off, a window was darkened that had thrown its beams across all England" (*Defoe*, 276).

Literary and
Historical
Context

Defoe in the pillory.
After Eyre Crowe painting.

1

Crusoe and Defoe

Whenever I teach my large lecture course in the history of the English novel I ask my students how many have heard of *The Life and Strange Surprizing Adventures of Robinson Crusoe, of York, Mariner*. All have. When I ask whether any have read the book in its complete, original version many readily admit that they have not. What they know they have absorbed from the cultural residue of Crusoe's fame, or from shortened, edited, and expurgated children's versions of the novel, or from comic books, movies, even *New Yorker* cartoons. I then ask another question. Of those who have heard of *Crusoe* and have not read it in its original form, how many can describe the basic plot of the story? Again, the bare elements of Crusoe's story as island castaway are known by all, but the rest of the book is a blur. What happened to Crusoe before his shipwreck? Where is the book set? When did its events occur? What were the sequence of events on the island? What happened to Crusoe after his rescue? What place does *Robinson Crusoe* hold in the history and literary history of its own time? What was Daniel Defoe like?

The quality of the Crusoe myth, its seeming absorption into the culture as one of its founding stories, is both an advantage and a disadvantage in thinking about the complete original version of Defoe's novel. Reading the book as Defoe wrote it challenges students in a number of ways they may not have anticipated or suspected. For one thing, the narrative in its fullness introduces matters of wide and complex appeal that are not always as familiar as the rudiments of the castaway plot: speculations on maritime and international law, on plantation husbandry, on slavery and cannibalism, on economic theory. For another, Defoe is a figure of fearless engagement with his age and boundless energies that are worth studying in conjunction with his famous castaway story. Here is the way the *Weekly Journal, or British Gazetteer* reacted to Defoe on 8 November 1718, the year before *Crusoe*. The squib lampoons his checkered career as a linen factor, tile manufacturer, itinerant spy, perfumer, merchant adventurer, ship owner, embezzler, bankrupt, and professional liar.

> To fraud his nature did his thoughts dispose,
> Since prentice to the trade of selling hose;
> And having furbisht up a stock of wiles,
> Mankind he cheated next by bricks and tiles:
> Bought coach and horses, but for none did pay,
> Nor one brass farthing for his corn and hay:
> And in like manner to conceal his shame,
> Bought civet cats to scent a stinking name:
> And finding that his ship would run aground,
> March'd quickly off with fifteen hundred pound . . .
> This wretch if possible will cheat Old Nick,
> He's so inur'd to fraudulence and trick.
> Great Bulzebube himself he does outvie
> For malice, treachery, and audacious lye.

When asked what he did for a living, Defoe always considered himself a simple tradesman. And in a way he was right, though he was surely a bit of everything else the lampoon charged. He lived what he referred to metaphorically in various autobiographical fragments as a life of shipwreck and recovery, going belly up for the first time when his merchant ship named, like Tennessee Williams's streetcar, *Desire* fell to pirates. Defoe took risks, suffered from them, and invariably bounced back for more. In sum, he was one of the most experienced, savvy, and innovative participants in eighteenth-century life, and, whether a merchant or a writer, always in the business of selling himself. The *Crusoe* saga is not merely the tale of an island castaway but of a commercial adventurer whose product, like Defoe's, is endurance. One of my goals in this volume is to emphasize the force of character in this wonderful book, to chart not only the strange and remote quality of *Robinson Crusoe* but the special contours of Defoe's extraordinary imagination, which draws so powerfully from his own varied experience in his own time.

As a mirror of contemporary issues and pressures, the novel form had no sustaining practitioner before Defoe to boost it to a place in the literary hierarchy. Shoddily written fictional true-to-life accounts existed in the culture much like the flotsam and jetsam of Crusoe's shipwreck before he fashioned his coherent island estate. And, of course, preexisting narrative forms of epic and romance, those deriving from classical sources in Greece and Rome or from aristocratic feudal cultures of medieval and Renaissance Europe, existed as timeworn narrative models. But these proved unsuitable for Defoe's charting of the contemporary record, his documentation and inscription of life in the late seventeenth and early eighteenth centuries, perhaps because none was able to do what the last great epic work in England, Milton's *Paradise Lost,* did: combine a compelling narrative event with the awakening reality of individual conscience in modern society.

The literary challenge for Defoe, and, to be accurate, not all writers conceived of the challenge as worthy, was to rework Milton's epic of conscience into the novelistic domain of social and material reality. Defoe was powerfully positioned to do so. In a varied course that took him from palace halls to prison cells, he registered the age's temper and tone, and he worried his head over everything from the herring fishing grounds off the coast of Scotland to the navigable rivers of the Congo, from the cost of wine to the national debt, from toll roads to moon flights, from the tenure of kings to local politics in the Palatinate. He advised monarchs in open counsel and he spied for ministers in close retreat. He served as the editorial voice of a government and he was a mole in the rival newspaper offices of political parties. He pondered phenomena from the appearance of ghosts to the meteorological mysteries of storms. He entertained schemes for a range of projects from diving engines to recover buried treasure to systematic workman's compensation and social security programs, from women's education to road repair. He ran factories, imported wine, floated insurance schemes, cluttered the civil and criminal courts with lawsuits. He negotiated treaties, traded extensively, and published voluminously.

Moreover, from his early days at Morton's Dissenting Academy, he was a quick read, studying widely in history, physical science, geography, natural and civil law, theology, and literature. These interests never abated; in fact, he made use of his writing career to expand the areas in which he could, with justification, claim expertise. He wrote for money, but he also wrote to cultivate his own knowledge in subjects that fascinated him. As a journalist and as a novelist, Defoe believed that writing was connected in basic ways to observing, witnessing, presenting, or laying out a scene and its particulars. What individuals filtered through their minds, what they saw, thought, desired, feared, and recorded was describable and knowable. The unique individual perception of both material circumstance and social reality appealed to Defoe, as it did to some of his famous contemporaries: Isaac Newton in science, John Locke in psychology and political theory, and William Petty in economics.

At the time he wrote *Crusoe*, in 1719, Defoe was nearly sixty and working for the ascendant Whig political party in England. To grasp the major project of Defoe's enormously prolific writing career is to understand the progression during his life from Restoration England, a period subject to the fading dynastic pressures of absolute monarchical rule, to a modern, mercantile, Parliamentary England flourishing in the midst of global commercial and imperial expansion. Robinson Crusoe, none too coincidentally, returns home to England just before the 1688 Bloodless Revolution, a moment Defoe saw as the fulcrum point of his own and his nation's history, a moment that marked the shift between old and new orders. The Revolution that dismissed the Stuart kings and eventually brought the Hanoverian succession to England also brought Daniel Defoe to the fore as a major writer in support of a new national vision: legal, balanced, tolerant government at home and colonial merchant adventurism abroad. After 1688, England entered a brave new world under a rational king, William III, whom Defoe served as counselor and civil servant. That Crusoe returns at a time when Defoe could and did exercise his best vision in an island state, an England drawing on the common interests of its individual citizens during the dawn of its commercial civilization, should not be lost on Defoe's readers. These concerns frame the *Crusoe* story, and in the course of the following chapters I hope to show how many other aspects of this universal, almost mythic book are commensurate with the historical and literary pressures that generated it.

2

The Importance of the Work

Some books hold central places and register key values in the history of a culture, whether or not they are actually read in their original or complete versions. They possess an aura, having been absorbed into cultural memory in a way that transcends even the lure of their details. The Bible is such a book; so, too, the Homeric *Odyssey*, Melville's *Moby-Dick*, or Twain's *Huckleberry Finn*. These works, and Daniel Defoe's *Robinson Crusoe* is among them, enjoy the cultural privilege of acquaintance before a reader engages the special pleasures afforded by reading them.

The centrality of the Crusoe story in the collective mind of this culture—indeed, in the collective mind of so many of the world's cultures—is astounding. Perhaps no single book in the history of Western literature has spawned more editions, translations, imitations, continuations, and sequels than *Crusoe*. To follow its paper trail over the centuries is an adventure almost as daunting as the one Crusoe faces on his island. There have been hundreds of adaptations in dozens of languages, from *Swiss Family Robinson*, to an Offenbach operetta, to Luis Buñuel's brilliant film version, to J. M. Coetzee's *Foe*. Crusoe's adventures form the basis of everything from a jokebook to a cookbook; he even appears in animal narratives as a dog. By the end of the nineteenth century, English language editions alone topped two hundred, with editions of translations abroad multiplying that number threefold. Any book translated into languages as remote from one another as Eskimo, Coptic, and Maltese must be making a deep impression on someone.

In terms of what opinion polls call recognition factor, Crusoe's name is magic. The castaway Crusoe appears everywhere, from Karl Marx's *Das Kapital* to television ads for permanent-press slacks. What is the appeal of his archetypal story? Is a man alone, stranded, outcast, exiled on a temperate desert island somehow an emblem of the organizing capacities of mind and body? How does a human being in isolation combine the resources of nature and culture? What does the mastery of spatial domain have to do with well-being? What does the lone individual need? These questions are so basic that *Robinson Crusoe* is a primer for the science of man, a field study for the anthropologist, the psychologist, the economist, the political scientist, the sociologist, the geographer, the engineer, the agronomist, the theologian, and even, as the story develops, the military strategist.

Crusoe's experience, as Samuel Taylor Coleridge put it, is a staple of fantasy projection, "a vision of a happy nightmare."[1] A soul alone on a desert island turns to self-generated resources; free space and free time provide for the disposition of material life and for the release of psychic energies. Defoe, of course, is aware of the psychological appeal of his narrative. Here, for example, are a few sentences as Crusoe explores an inland paradise on his island, much more lovely and beautiful a place than his settlement nearer the shore: "I descended a little of the Side of that delicious Vale, surveying it with a secret Kind of Pleasure, (tho-mixt with my other afflicting Thoughts) to think that this was all my own, that I was King and Lord of all this Country indefeasibly, and had a Right of Possession; and if I could convey it, I might have it in Inheritance, as compleatly as any Lord of a Mannor in *England*" (100).

What does a secret kind of pleasure mean? The place is an island spot within an island setting—Crusoe loves enclosures within enclosures—and Crusoe's pleasure is an expression of subliminal and activated desires. He takes a piece of paradise and makes it a sovereign state. He is king of vale, lord of the country, squire of the manor. Visionary spots such as these are narcissistic and, as befits the dreams of the material man, owned, protected, held. Crusoe's pleasure in paradise has something of the same relation to the rest of his life as Defoe's novel has to the lives of those who read it. The imagination seeks its sovereign territories, its islanded fictions, and Defoe works that notion into his extraordinary story for all it is worth.

Crusoe's story is a fable of controlling physical space, of organizing time, of making, crafting, fabricating, of fearing and mastering. His fate and his opportunity touch a responsive chord in all those who ponder the course of a life and value the appeal of alternative or substitute worlds. As Crusoe remakes himself in a space that he inscribes, that space becomes him. To think of the man is to think in terms of the whole phrase, "Crusoe on his island." Conjuring up an empty space and setting out its contours is therapeutic, satisfying, and liberating. Indeed, those in long captivity often sustain themselves by imagining an empty plot of land and building a house brick by brick or board by board in their mind's eye. As time goes by, they will landscape the space, possibly add an addition or create an entire compound. It is the rare human being who is not compelled by this kind of projection.

Crusoe's story is emblematic for the genre of the novel in England, which Defoe's narrative, in a sense, inaugurated. When James Joyce, a novelist who militantly adapted or readapted the heroic course of Western narrative into the modified domain of the bourgeois hero, wonders in a refrain from *Ulysses*, "*O, poor Robinson Crusoe, / How could you possibly do so?*",[2] he asks a question, in a sense, about the book's place in literary history. For Joyce, Defoe's Crusoe is the "English Ulysses," the westering hero with commercial ledger in hand, the man who wanders to the extremes of the world to experience what constitutes the daily texture of life. The displacement of the epic wanderer into localized fictional domain is the story of the novel's evolution. Further, when Joyce calls his own *Ulysses* the "allincluding" chronicle of the West he marks the path that detours from Homer through the English Ulysses to the Irish one, a path traveled by Defoe's merchant castaway and by his own ad man, Leopold Bloom, employed by an appropriately named *Freeman's Journal.* The first free man's journal in the modern novel belongs to Crusoe on his island.

What Joyce saw in Defoe's *Crusoe* is a radical experiment in narrative-mythic form: myth located in the bedrock of physical space and local artifact. And what impressed Joyce about *Crusoe* is the total craft of the book, the craft that Crusoe displays on his island and the craft that Defoe displays in making Crusoe. *Robinson Crusoe* is not spun of the stuff of marvelous invention but fabricated, built, put together as real, as natural, as painstaking. Joyce understands, as did Defoe, that the greatest powers of fictional imagination reside in the most rigorous and deliberate powers of fictional reconstruction. And Joyce recognizes that in *Robinson Crusoe* resides the history of the novel "like the soul that slumbers in an imperfect and amorphous organism."[3] Joyce's words at the conclusion of a lecture on Defoe are eloquent:

> The story of the shipwrecked sailor who lived on the desert island reveals, as perhaps no other book throughout the long history of English literature does, the wary and heroic instinct of the rational animal and the prophecy of the empire. . . . The true symbol of the British conquest is Robinson Crusoe, who, cast away on a desert island, in his pocket a knife and a pipe, becomes an architect, a carpenter, a knifegrinder, an astronomer, a baker, a shipwright, a potter, a saddler, a farmer, a tailor, an umbrella-maker, and a clergyman. He is the true prototype of the British colonist, as Friday (the trusty savage who arrives on an unlucky day) is the symbol of the subject races. The whole Anglo-Saxon spirit is in Crusoe: the manly independence; the unconscious cruelty; the persistence; the slow yet efficient intelligence; the sexual apathy; the practical, well-balanced religiousness; the calculating taciturnity. Whoever rereads this simple, moving book in the light of subsequent history cannot help but fall under its prophetic spell.

Saint John the Evangelist saw on the island of Patmos the apocalyptic ruin of the universe and the building of the walls of the eternal city sparkling with beryl and emerald, with onyx and jasper, with sapphire and ruby. Crusoe saw only one marvel in all the fertile creation around him, the print of a naked foot in the virgin sand. And who knows if the latter is not more significant than the former? (24–25)

3

Critical Reception

The form of the novel in England did not burst into existence solely as the imp of Defoe's genius, though it might appear so. For decades the later seventeenth and earlier eighteenth century struggled to find a form of literary expression in which some of the strong fervor of contemporary historical events, domestic consciousness, social analysis, and the new psychology of John Locke and others might manifest itself. When in his late fifties Defoe began writing volumes of fiction that did a little of all these things, the English could not even find an adequate name for his narratives. Novel was the last thing anyone would call Defoe's works. In point of fact, the term *novel* usually referred to the stylized, ornate, and time-distanced French romance. The circumstantially particularized, recognizable, and roughly contemporary stories Defoe told, beginning with *Robinson Crusoe* and continuing with *Memoirs of a Cavalier, Moll Flanders, Colonel Jack,* and *Roxana,* were a conglomerate of lives, confessions, memoirs, accounts, true histories, and diaries.

"The editor," writes Defoe in the preface to *Crusoe,* "believes the thing to be a just History of Fact; neither is there any Appearance of Fiction in it" (1). He means what he says—the whole may indeed be fiction, but there is no "appearance" of fiction in it. Appearances are what count for Defoe. The distinction between something being a lie and something appearing to be a lie holds a world of difference. The truth is not the record of what happened merely, but the believability of the mode of writing that conveys it, or something like it. The writing can be true and the events fiction. That is why the editor believes there is "no appearance" of fiction in the writing; he is making a stylistic comment as much as a judgment about content. And that is why *Crusoe* comes down through the centuries as special and novel, though only well after Defoe and most of his contemporaries were dead would critics call his works what he himself would have shuddered to call them, novels.

Robinson Crusoe did not address itself at first to an audience well schooled in how to read it as fiction. It passed itself off as a counterfeit memoir and was published by a house that specialized in everything but fiction. The publisher of *Crusoe,* W. Tayler at the sign of the Ship in Pater Noster Row, included in the first printing of Defoe's book a select listings of titles in his house. These tell something of what he hoped to sell to those who, presumably, were reading *Crusoe.* More important, when Defoe came out with the sequel to his book, *The Farther Adventures of Robinson Crusoe* (1719), Tayler inserted a thirty-page catalog of his entire list at the end of the printed text, nearly two hundred titles.

Both lists are fascinating. The only other contemporary works that could be called novels are Defoe's own forthcoming *Memoirs of a Cavalier* (1720) and the first volume of *Robinson Crusoe* (both advertised in the sequel). There is one contemporary romance, *The New Atlantis.* The listing of classics is minimal, mostly Plutarch and Ovid but only a few titles for each. Far and away the bulk of the books listed, over sixty for the two volumes, are on religious subjects or religious histories, from Bishop Taylor's *Holy Living and Dying* to Swinden's *An Enquiry into the Nature and Place of Hell.* English and European history, geography, and travel are next at thirty-five volumes. There are twenty-two volumes on contemporary English poetry and drama and the same number on practical information books (technical books, dictionaries, practical handbooks on various subjects). Science books number eleven. There is one conduct book, an appropriate one for Crusoe, *Advice to a Son, Directing how to Demean himself in the most Important Affairs of Life.*

Tayler's list is typical for the decade in which *Crusoe* appeared. Readers in 1719 wanted to know about science and the practical realities of their world, but, mostly, they wanted to know about the state of their souls and about what writers thought about the state of everybody else's soul. To read *Robinson Crusoe* as a memoir of spiritual conversion, as the rooting out of sinful and disobedient inclinations, is not odd in this light and many still read it as such.[4] In the preface of *The Farther Adventures*, Defoe claims that he considered Crusoe's secular story an occasion to draw on both religious and historical fables to supplement the meaning of Crusoe's adventure: "The just application of every Incident, the religious and useful Inferences drawn from every Part, are so many Testimonies to the good Design of making it publick, and must legitimate all the Part that may be call'd Invention, or Parable in the Story" (*Works*, 2:i). As is often the case, Defoe plays a bit here with truth and fiction. He takes testimonies to acknowledge the usefulness of lies, but readers get religion in Defoe the same way they get history, by interpreting the details of someone's story.

Defoe's introduction of fictional material into a world eager to read about moral designs for life and practical information for living allows his readers to partake of two worlds, one potentially oriented toward the higher plane of applied moral meaning and the other toward the circumstantial phenomena of recognizable daily living. These, none too coincidentally, mimic the range of books his publisher, W. Tayler, had in stock. Defoe knew that the bedrock of fictional narration was to make the fiction appear to be a true relation, and it is fitting that if Tayler chose to publish a book about a castaway English merchant adventurer who constructs a habitable estate on an isolated island, he would also choose to advertise books that range from Boetius's *Consolation of Philosophy* to Dr. J. S.'s *The Way to be Wise and Wealthy; or, The Excellency of Industry and Frugality, etc. Recommended in particular to the Gentleman, Scholar, Soldier, Trader, Sailor, Artificer, and Husbandman.* Crusoe would do well to own other books on Tayler's list. As cartographer, he could use *The Country Gentleman's Vade Mecum, Whole Art of Surveying and Measuring Land.* As botanist, he could employ *English Herbal; or, History of Plants in alphabetical order.* As merchant adventurer, *Lex Mercatoria; or, The Laws relating to Commerce.* As geographer, *A Treatise of both Globes. To which is added, A Geographical Description of our Earth.* The readers for whom Crusoe's story was targeted knew about many things, and they may well have thought their knowledge of Crusoe's plight supplemented the knowledge of the real world they already possessed. The intricacies and ironies of modern prose fiction were not matters that overly concerned the first readers of Defoe's famous story.

Whatever Defoe's first readers thought they were getting in *Crusoe,* they read it with fervor. The narrative was something of a landmark text within a year of its publication. Its first issue of between 1,000 and 1,500 copies, entered in the Stationers' Register for 23 April 1719 and available two days later, quickly sold out even at the relatively high price of five shillings. Defoe's bilious enemy, Charles Gildon, commented soon after *Crusoe*'s publication, "There is not an old Woman that can go to the Price of it, but buys thy Life and Adventures, and leaves it as a Legacy, with the *Pilgrims Progress,* the *Practice of Piety,* and *God's Revenge against Murther,* to her Posterity."[5] Before the end of the year, the first volume of *Crusoe* had run through four editions, 12 May, 6 June, and 8 August, each with multiple issues. By 1722, Tayler printed the sixth edition of the first part of the *Crusoe* saga with maps and plates. The volume still bore a premium price, which means the volumes were holding their own in the market. The second part, *The Farther Adventures of Robinson Crusoe,* appeared hard upon the first on 17 August 1719 (with another edition that same year), and the last volume, *Serious Reflections during the Life and Surprising Adventures of Robinson*

Crusoe, a reflection upon the writing and moral nature of the novel, appeared a year later, 3 August 1720.

There were no subsequent editions under Tayler's imprint. Three complete piracies of the text in cheap editions, including a Dublin piracy under the imprint of an appropriately named G. Risk, appeared in the first year of *Crusoe*'s publication. In addition, a serialized piracy of the story began as early as 7 October 1719 in the *Original London Post: or, Heathcot's Intelligence.* Tayler fended off these piracies as best he could for a few years by reprinting the volumes in new editions and reissues. In 1724, after Tayler's death, Thomas Longman, of the publishing house that has lasted through the centuries, bought out much of Tayler's stock and controlled the rights to *Robinson Crusoe,* insofar as numerous piracies and abridgements through the 1720s and 1730s allowed.

Determining the effect of a book is not merely a matter of counting the copies sold, though Defoe's bookseller surely did that and reacted accordingly. The impact can also be measured by the breadth of awareness, by extracts, piracies, foreign editions, and translations, by the range of response in intellectual circles, in coffeehouse society, in manorial kitchens, and in town house salons. On this basis, and within a matter of decades, *Robinson Crusoe* had reached an audience as wide as any book ever written in English. It had become a part of the literary consciousness of European civilization, a favorite work of such diverse figures as Cotton Mather, Jean-Jacques Rousseau, Benjamin Franklin, and Samuel Johnson. Johnson put it in a very special category: "Was there anything yet written by mere man that was wished longer by its readers, excepting *Don Quixote, Robinson Crusoe, Pilgrim's Progress?*"[6]

Part of any great work's legacy is the degree to which other works of genius are based upon its premise, even if that premise becomes the grounds for a systematic critique of its values. Such was the case almost immediately for *Robinson Crusoe* in that Jonathan Swift's great narrative, *Gulliver's Travels,* required Robinson Crusoe's fame for the experiences of his own Lemuel Gulliver to carry full satiric force. Swift charts in Defoe's *Crusoe* a kind of formalized egomania, and Gulliver is a Crusoe figure who comes apart at the subjective seams, an adventurer whose ego destroys him, whose self-absorption is a mental travesty, whose compulsion is a human failing, whose neuroses take him right out of body and mind. Gulliver is doomed from the beginning because he traffics in all the goods that make up Defoe's new store for narrative—obsessive realism, mindless psychologizing, inordinate detail, self-valorization.

Indeed, one of the measures of the success of Defoe's fictional experiment in *Crusoe* is the degree to which conserving and suspicious satirists, such as Jonathan Swift, went in abusing him. Near the beginning of *Gulliver's Travels,* Swift talks casually of hosiers, a pointed reference to Defoe's early occupation, and of Newgate Street, Defoe's notorious prison address. *Gulliver's Travels* is a version of what happens when those like Defoe, whom Swift called the "new men," presume to elevate into literary life the middling, domestic, and material values of eighteenth-century life. Even before *Gulliver's Travels* Swift had attacked Defoe's "mock authoritative Manner."[7] The audience Defoe addresses, the tone he takes, and the agenda of middle-class, individualist ascendancy struck Swift as inflated and disfiguring.

What is at issue between Defoe and Swift is the state of the modern mind and the relation of that mind to the practices of early eighteenth-century prose fiction. Swift's attack on the premises of *Robinson Crusoe* is essentially an attack on the premises of the early novel. Though Swift had no full comprehension, nor did Defoe at the time, of how that form would develop, the tendencies Swift saw he despised. If *Robinson Crusoe* explores the nature of a sovereign individual in a world of his own making, its subject is very close to those the novel will generally develop as it matures through the century. Precisely the coming of age of a new focus in narrative, a focus on the exigencies of daily living, on the trials of the commercial or urban victim, appalled Swift. He saw such narrative innovation as the ruination of literary sensibility.

Critical Reception

All that Defoe strives to accomplish in writing Crusoe onto his island Swift attempts to demolish in his satiric world of private madness. He wreaks havoc with the self-image so important to Robinson Crusoe by destroying the fictional contract that sets the self in a recognizable world. He makes people too little and too big in *Gulliver's Travels;* he makes landed forms fly; he makes horses talk. He takes away the notion of security generated from material reality, the notion that the narrative imagination makes its own serviceable fiction and keeps that fiction consistent within the realm of probability. The supremely modern and confident Gulliver is made to feel alien to himself, all bent out of shape, as if he is another creature. He suffers from a failure of nerve and imagination in situations where Crusoe thrives. At the end of his narrative Gulliver is a hater of his species, a traveler whose names for things come from the language of horses. The parallel and undermining of Defoe's famous castaway is telling and definitive:

> My Design was, if possible, to discover some small Island unin-
> habited, yet sufficient by my Labour to furnish me with Necessaries
> of Life, which I would have thought a greater Happiness than to
> be first Minister in the politest Court of *Europe;* so horrible was
> the Idea I conceived of returning to live in the Society and under
> the Government of *Yahoos.* For in such a Solitude as I desired, I
> could at least enjoy my own Thoughts, and reflect with Delight on
> the Virtues of those inimitable *Houyhnhnms,* without any Oppor-
> tunity of degenerating into the Vices and Corruptions of my own
> Species.[8]

But soon after Gulliver sets foot on such an island in his adventures he is shot in the knee with an arrow by the hostile natives. He escapes in despair aboard a Portuguese trading vessel. This is to dismiss Defoe's island fable in a few paragraphs. The attack on *Crusoe* is pointed, though the only thing that Swift fails to understand is the sustaining power of the realistic narrative form he decries and the role that form will play in the next three hundred years of literary history.

19

For centuries now it seems writers have been writing into the interstices of the Crusoe story or, more intriguingly, retelling the story from perspectives other than Defoe's original. Michel Tournier's *Friday* and J. M. Coetzee's *Foe* are among the best of these attempts. Coetzee especially tells a pressing story of colonial misrepresentation: Friday has no tongue; Robinson has rotten teeth, neglected by twenty-eight years of not flossing; and, lo and behold, a woman on the island, Susan Barton, casts severe doubt on Crusoe's powers of recollection, not to mention his sexual abstinence. Very little in Defoe's version remains the same. Crusoe lies about his past, about the sequence surrounding Friday's arrival, about his penchant for journal writing, about his desire for renewed social conversation, about the whole complex experience of island life.

Coetzee's tactic in challenging Crusoe's reliability seems a modern one, but he knows enough of the history of the book he rewrites to recognize that from the very beginning at least one critic was on Crusoe's case, and by implication, Defoe's, for lying. Shortly after the publication of *Robinson Crusoe*, Charles Gildon, an insufferable hack critic, figured he had spotted a ruse. In his *The Life and Strange Surprizing Adventures of Mr. D - - - - - De F - -, of London, Hosier* (1719), he surmised that Crusoe was invented out of whole cloth. Defoe already had a reputation as a liar for his journalistic ventures. Just before the writing of *Robinson Crusoe*, J. Read's *Weekly Journal*, 8 November 1718, included an attack on Defoe's skullduggery: "there need no other Proof of his binomial Performance, than the agreeableness of the stile and manner; the little Art he is truly Master of, of forging a Story and imposing it on the World for Truth."

The anonymous writer of this letter employs "forging" in the sense of counterfeiting, but forge can mean "to make" as well as "to fake" in the same way that James Joyce employs the word at the end of *Portrait of the Artist* when Stephen Dedalus uses the little art he possesses to "forge within the smithy" of his soul the conscience of his race. Whereas some of his contemporaries were upset by Defoe's lying, and whereas Coetzee is amused, Defoe is emboldened by the idea of fiction as a made truth. That is perhaps why he was so quick to claim in *Serious Reflections during the Life and Surprising Adventures of Robinson Crusoe* that anyone who denies the character denies the book, and Defoe makes his claim by turning around the very charge leveled against him by his early readers—that he is a liar: "I *Robinson Crusoe,* being at this time in perfect and sound mind and memory, thanks be to God therefor, do hereby declare their objection is an invention scandalous in design, and false in fact; and do affirm that the story, though allegorical, is also historical; and that it is the beautiful representation of a life of unexampled misfortune, and of a variety not to be met with in the world" (*Works,* 3:ix).

What could Defoe mean by this phrasing? He knows Crusoe does not exist and says as much in a few paragraphs, hinting that all events in fiction are real insofar as they exist as the "borrow'd Lights" of some interpretable story or another. But to call Crusoe a lie is to intimate that the process of fiction is incapable of producing an experience that, because it seems so true and powerful, is, in a sense, real. Defoe could not abide the notion that narrative invention is primarily a lie; it is, instead, a carefully crafted simulacrum, a stand-in for or mimicry of truth whose value resides in its *as if* quality.

Defoe seems to want to say that the usual distinctions made about fictionality do not apply in his case, and, indeed, they do not. He is at great pains in his *Reflections* to isolate kinds of truth, psychological from actual, realistic from factual, circumstantial from corroborative. In his clumsy grappling with his first naive critics, Defoe was beginning to form a basis for the defense of realism in fiction. That defense was sustained in some measure by every novelist worth his or her salt after him, and by critics through the nineteenth and twentieth centuries, from Coleridge to Georg Lukács. The artistic nature of realism and Defoe's speculations about what he was trying to accomplish in the *Crusoe* saga are essential to the understanding of the new literary form he helped design and develop.

Of course, early readers like Gildon worry less about the techniques of novelistic impersonation and story telling than about the abuses Defoe has perpetrated on a receptive audience. For Defoe to mask the economic wreck of his life in *Crusoe,* as Gildon charges in *The Life and Strange Surprizing Adventures of Mr. D - - - - - De F - -, of London, Hosier,* is the worst of fictional illegitimacies. Legitimate travel experiences are one thing; adventures fabricated out of thin air are another. A travel memoir in which bogus adventures are substituted for the exigencies of one's life is trash. Gildon's objection reveals a basic dilemma for readers of Defoe's fiction. What is the status of something that claims to be real and yet is recognized as serving other potential realities? Or of something that exchanges one realistic pattern of circumstantial reality for another implied and hidden one? Gildon made his charges against *Robinson Crusoe* without a fully developed sense of the flexibility and variety of realism in fiction, but his question still haunts a good deal of Defoe criticism today.[9]

Gildon attacked on the basis of an unexamined assumption that writers of fiction should not be pretenders to true historical writing. Those writing in the memoir tradition, those recording lives and adventures, those mapping travels have precious little leeway to invent, especially when the invention of one set of facts serves to sneak in another. But he fails or refuses to see that Defoe is writing a different kind of novel than had ever been written before, that realism is never a simple or simpleminded substitution of pretense for fact but a full imitative circumstantial scene that provides new contexts for interpreting the psychological and material pressures of reality. Precisely because Defoe could write a fully convincing and detailed rendering of the life of a shipwrecked adventurer on a remote island he could also draw into his fable parallel topics and issues ranging from personal biography to natural law, economic theory, religious conversion, colonial policy, and animal and plant husbandry.

The question that critics ought to have asked, if they had the critical wherewithal to ask it or if the form in which Defoe was working had a more pronounced history, was much more daring: What is a novel? In 1719 this was not an easy question; perhaps it is not an easy question now, but, at least, some of Defoe's work has made it a different question. An early reader such as Charles Gildon simply did not recognize the complexity of his reaction to *Crusoe*, though, curiously, Gildon guessed at its interpretable qualities and, more important, guessed that the texture of reality created in it was the beginning of an important experiment in narrative. Defoe was setting new relations between the claims made by history and those made by fiction. The mask of truth may be the strangest fiction of all, and the best fiction may masquerade as something quite different from invention.

If Gildon had worked closely with the text and style of *Crusoe*, he might have been able to lay out his charges with more intriguing evidence about what it is Defoe's realism accomplishes in fictionalizing the incidents of one man's life in another's. But it was not until the nineteenth century that the shrewd criticism of William Hazlitt and Samuel Taylor Coleridge seriously explored the techniques Defoe developed for lying while seeming to tell the truth. These are still matters of supreme interest to the current crop of Defoe's critics, who focus their attention on the complementary topics of Defoe's realism and the fictional worlds produced by his various and remarkably inventive mind.

A Reading

4

Robinson Crusoe and the Theory of the Novel

The literary revolution that Defoe's *Robinson Crusoe* helped instigate is monumental. No matter what talk there is of the forebears of the novel, very little reads like a novel until Defoe develops the form beginning with *Crusoe* and continuing through the 1720s with *Moll Flanders, Colonel Jack,* and *Roxana.* Surely, there are elements in previous English works, from Thomas Nashe's *Unfortunate Traveler* to Aphra Behn's *Oronooko* to William Congreve's *Incognita,* that suggest novelistic tendencies, but each of these still reads as if it is something else, a rogue's narrative, a heroic romance, a salon romance. Defoe's early novels appear as though they are actually the things they pretend to be, bona fide memoirs, confessions, histories. They have the feel of circumstantial and psychological realism to them, two of the qualifying attributes for the genre Defoe was so instrumental in developing.

Over the years, those writing on Defoe have tried to link his narrative experiments to conventional real-life forms, primarily the memoir, the spiritual autobiography, and the personal conduct book. Surely, there is considerable reason for doing so. Defoe had trained early in these forms and in the circumstantial realism that was to mark them. His first full-length narrative work, *The Storm* (1704), a rendering of the effects on individuals, physical and psychological,

27

of a vicious storm in the British isles, was but one of a number of accounts of contemporary life he chronicled for a reading public fascinated by the taking of testimony, the witnessing of unusual events, the moral and religious lessons to be learned from individual experiences and natural phenomena.

For twenty years before the writing of *Crusoe* Defoe was an accomplished, talented, and fecund journalist. He knew what his contemporaries had on their minds just as he knew his age's stories, listened to its conversations, and pondered its events. It is in no small measure from Defoe's journalistic training that his interests as a narrative artist derive and that his style evolves, a style geared to making the social, economic, and psychological circumstances of his time comprehensible to reasonably educated men and women. He wrote about everything that took place in English life, from religious scandals to money kiting schemes, from the misery of bankrupts to the benefits of island trade, from parish politics to foreign wars, from family imbroglios to state politics.

For years he was remarkably inventive in figuring ways to package information and deliver it. The body of Defoe's journalism is invaded by small narrative microbes, conversational set pieces, overheard anecdotes, even heartrending pleas for missing persons and ingenious ads for a range of bizarre goods from trusses to venereal elixirs. To read the hundreds of mininarratives that accompany his periodical articles, features, and columns is to recognize that his imagination is essentially illustrative. His journalistic prose is rife with epiphanies of English life. Defoe could never resist a good story, and he never forgot one. James Sutherland claims that *Robinson Crusoe* was written for the same readers that read Defoe's prose and journalism for many years: "Defoe was reaching a new public; it might even be said that he was creating one."[10]

Those who have read through Defoe's voluminous journalism and public writing argue that it is not only possible to derive from his work the run of his opinions on virtually every issue that concerned the English for decades, but the run of everyone else's opinions as well, whether or not Defoe agreed with them. Within Defoe's diffuse and multiple voicings, his constant counterfeiting of a chorus of different personalities, groups, professions, classes, it is possible to hear at one time or another almost every vernacular twist and turn in the land. In a famous letter to Robert Harley, whom Defoe served as a spy, Defoe hints at something of the technique that sustained him for years as a journalist and would sustain him, in later years, as a novelist: "I Talk to Everybody in Their Own way."[11] By this Defoe means that he approaches different groups of people in terms of their own interests, but he also centers his capacity for mimicry and impersonation that, in a Keatsian sense, is a power of genius, a capacity of voicing otherness that some call lying or fiction writing. James Sutherland again makes a connection that serves Defoe's novels: "he was moving about from day to day among people who mistook him for someone else; he had a secret to keep, a little world of make-believe to wander in. But above all—and this was the very breath of life to Defoe—he had his finger in every man's pie" (*Defoe*, 150).

Defoe had a vocational reason as a government spy for writing himself into another voice, but he was a born mimic almost by impulse. When he told stories in other voices, he told them with fervor, as if they were absolutely true, absolutely genuine. The difference for Defoe between the pose of truth and actual truth is one of degree not kind. In this sense, Defoe did not so much sit down late in his life to invent the novel with works such as *Crusoe* and *Memoirs of a Cavalier* as he did to supplement the literature of true relation with a literature very like true relation. He followed this procedure exactly in his *History of the Pyrates* (1724), where it is difficult to distinguish between the lives of real pirates who sailed the seven seas and the lives of counterfeit pirates Defoe made up to bulk out his narrative. It is credibility that makes an impression for Defoe, and verification is something of a fool's errand.

Defoe's theory of representation—if it can be so called—is very much keyed to the notion of probable circumstance. He makes a greater distinction between the likely and the marvelous than between the factual and fictional. When Robinson Crusoe, storm-tossed by waves before being cast on his island's shore, asks himself a question he inadvertently asks a key question about the narrative he is in: "how was it possible I could get on Shore?" (46). The question Crusoe poses about the action is indeed the question at the heart of Defoe's fictional enterprise. How does he make events appear possible?

Perhaps Samuel Coleridge puts his finger on the answer when he says of *Crusoe* in comparison with virtually all else delivered under the guise of fiction before it: it has "the *desert island* feeling" (Coleridge, 161). It is worth pondering for a moment what Coleridge might mean here. Is he thinking about the texture of the experience or the texture of the writing? Or of both? When Defoe defends his fiction in Crusoe's voice he does so on the basis that its writing feels circumstantially true, so much so that the island experience takes precedence over anything it might stand for symbolically. The following passage contains Defoe's theory of fiction all compressed. Its last sentence is a clinching argument. A reader need merely reverse its premises to get from Crusoe's experience back to Defoe's version of *Crusoe* as a true relation and supreme fiction.

> In like Manner, when in these Reflections, I speak of the Times and Circumstances of particular Actions done, or Incidents which happened in my Solitude and Island-Life, an impartial Reader will be so just to take it as it is; *viz.* that it is spoken or intended of that Part of the real Story, which the Island-Life is a just Allusion to; and in this the Story is not only illustrated, but the real Part I think most justly approv'd: *For Example,* in the latter Part of this Work called the Vision, I begin this, *When I was in my Island Kingdom, I had abundance of strange Notions of my seeing Apparitions,* &c. all these Reflections are just History of a State of forc'd Confinement, which in my real History is represented by a confin'd Retreat in an Island; and 'tis as reasonable to represent one kind of Imprisonment by another, as it is to represent any Thing that really exists, by that which exists not. (*Works,* 3:xii)

Robinson Crusoe and The Theory of the Novel

Here is a potent theory of realism within the new novelistic mode. It is clear that Defoe understands that truth in writing is not identical to truth in occurrence, but that there can be a validity and a verisimilitude that makes for a new reality, the reality of reading and believing something to be true because of the justice of its presentation. Truth is an aura not a fact. All of the potentialities of a new form, the realistic novel, are present in Defoe's defense of Crusoe's voice and experience: subjective certainty, circumstantial probability, psychological accuracy, temporal and spatial recognizability, and contemporary speech patterns and inflections. Further, Defoe's realistic characters acknowledge the active, decision-making stake human beings have in the contingent world. He does not write his characters into the prototypes of epic or romance situations in which behavior tends to be excessively coded and conventionalized, but into "the Times and Circumstances of particular Actions done." To put it another way, Defoe's characters face difficulties and encounter opportunities that, by a stretch of the imagination, could present themselves to many others in his reading audience.

The first sentence of the preface to *Robinson Crusoe*, "If ever the Story of any private Man's Adventures in the World were worth making Publick, and were acceptable when Publish'd, the Editor of this Account thinks this will be so" (1), could serve as a manifesto for the realistic novel, which would absorb the attention of readers, literary critics, and writers for the next three hundred years. It is only in the writing of the circumstantially private that Defoe understands the new space for the conventionally public. In Defoe's fiction, patterns of individual behavior are infinitely adjustable to circumstance. And the best record of those adjustments is the most satisfying depiction of those circumstances. Defoe's characters become archetypes of realistic fiction: Crusoe as Material Man; Colonel Jack as Itinerant Adventurer; Moll as Urban Survivor; Roxana as Middle-Class Femme Fatale. These made-up "true" adventures provide Defoe's readers with paradigms for living, choosing, valuing, judging, and appreciating.

For Defoe it is not just what Crusoe manipulates and arranges on his island that produces the book's realism, but what imprints itself on Crusoe's mind as well. It is possible to experience what is never even seen, which is one of the ways Defoe, in a wider context, will argue for the effect of realistic fiction. Crusoe has counter experiences on his island. That is, he imagines things. Here is a passage in which Crusoe's phrase "lively Colours" is Defoe's fictional shorthand for things impressed as probable into the topography of the fantasizing mind. Island life seems so real that Crusoe can imagine other versions of it: "I spent whole Hours, I may say whole Days, in representing to my self in the most lively Colours, how I must have acted, if I had got nothing out of the Ship. How I could not have so much as got any Food, except Fish and Turtles; and that as it was long before I found any of them, I must have perish'd first"(130).

Defoe reveals even more of his fictional hand when he writes in *Crusoe* about dreams felt to be real events. It is not that he believes the images of dreams actually take place outside the head, but that those images, much like the carefully fabricated fiction, make so powerful an impression they seem real. Of Crusoe's Avenging Angel dream, for example, Defoe implies that it has a kind of afterlife of its own; it is a real presence in Crusoe's memory: "nor is it any more possible to describe the Impression that remain'd upon my Mind when I awak'd and found it was but a Dream" (88). Presumably, readers of *Crusoe* might feel the same way about the entire island experience. They know Defoe imagined it, but its impression makes it mentally real for those reading it. Crusoe himself offers a few words on the realism of an impression, if not an event, when he speaks about his fantasy of killing cannibals: "my Invention now run quite another Way; for Night and Day, I could think of nothing but how I might destroy some of the Monsters in their cruel bloody Entertainment" (168). He tells us that "This Fancy pleas'd my Thoughts for some Weeks, and I was so full of it, that I often dream'd of it;

and sometimes that I was just going to let fly at them in my Sleep" (168–69).

In another dream scene from the narrative, Crusoe imagines Friday before Friday actually arrives. It is almost as if Crusoe knows that the likeliest candidate to serve as companion to him is one who reflects his own fears. In his dream, as in the fictional manifestation of Friday that follows it, Friday is about to be eaten when he is saved. It is not merely coincidental that the dream of Friday comes to him before the actual Friday. By thinking about it so strenuously he is ready to make it happen. Crusoe wants a Friday. Every Thursday, as James Joyce puts it, wants a Friday. An overplus of brain activity results in a dream discharge. A native runs toward a grove; Crusoe shows him his ladder; makes him his servant; wants his services as a pilot to get him off the island. All this is very quickly disposed in the narrative as a dream, almost as if the fantasy has to run its course quickly so that its realistic fulfillment can take place sooner.

The psychology of Defoe's realism conforms in its outlines to notions current in the later seventeenth and early eighteenth century about how the mind generates ideas and believes them to be true. John Locke's *Essay on Human Understanding* is the source of most of these notions, and Defoe is not above borrowing its concepts. Here is a typical Lockean passage in *Crusoe,* where the castaway, praying for companionship twenty-three years into his island life, experiences psychosomatic symptoms. The pressure of his praying hands "wou'd have crusht" any object involuntarily; and his teeth are so clenched he could not open his mouth. Then Defoe offers a bit of analysis that reflects the psychology of the early novel: "Let the Naturalists explain these Things, and the Reason and Manner of them; all I can say to them, is, to describe the Fact, which was even surprising to me when I found it; though I knew not from what it should proceed; it was doubtless the effect of ardent Wishes, and of strong Ideas form'd in my Mind" (188).

In a recent discovery of some of Defoe's earliest writings, dating back to the 1680s, Maximillian Novak came upon a manuscript labeled "Historical Collections; or, Memoirs of Passages & Stories." This is something of a young man's commonplace book, which amasses anecdotes and fables from literature and news stories or simple gossip circulating the town. They are brief but psychologically detailed and suggestive in a way that adumbrates Defoe's reliance later in his fiction on the power of psychological impression. For example, Defoe tells a story about a man so obsessed by a murder that he returns many years later to the place of a crime, when the event is largely forgotten, and confesses hysterically to having committed the deed. Those on the premises are perplexed. They have no reality in front of them and scarcely a memory behind them to work with. Defoe's point is that the impression of guilt is an inner impulse that reacts to circumstantial stimulus. The place reproduces the event. Guilt enters the mind and forms a subjective plot.

Defoe's later novels build on just such notions. The role the subjective force of character plays in setting the patterns, personal and historical, that generate fictional plots is one of his truly significant contributions to prose fiction. He is the first to welcome the full power of the realistic subjective voice in fiction. Crusoe's story, "represented to the World" as the "Life of a Man in an Island," is also about the solitary mind self-conceiving: "The World, I say, is nothing to us, but as it is more or less to our Relish: All Reflection is carry'd Home, and our Dear-self is, in one Respect, the End of Living" (Works, 3:4).

Late in Robinson Crusoe Defoe provides a telling instance of the subjective realism that controls the action. It occurs quickly and might be missed entirely, but it also reveals in a graphic way the extent to which subjective experience and fictional realism go hand in glove. An English captain, cast on the island by mutineers, is rescued by Crusoe and then has a thought: "but when he reflected from thence upon himself, and how I seem'd to have been preserv'd there, on purpose to save his Life, the Tears ran down his Face, and he could not speak a Word more" (258). To imagine that Crusoe, a being much like him, had been deposited on an island twenty-eight years for the express purpose of preserving him, who has been on it for a few hours, is to carry home all reflection with a vengeance. The assumption behind the captain's notion of events is extraordinary. But it is a productive assumption; it disposes the world's events for the individual experiencing them, and it sets the contours for subjective fictional representation.

The relevance of the subjective, self-centered fiction to the history of the novel remains clear up to the present century. Here, for example, is Marcel Proust on the idea of self-projection in life and in fiction: "Man is the creature who cannot escape from himself, who knows other people only in himself, and when he asserts the contrary, he is lying."[12] The connection between the impulse toward subjective reality and the circumstantial realism that surrounds such a reality draws a direct line from the origins of the novel with Defoe's *Crusoe* to its most complex and ornate formal expressions in the twentieth century.

5

Island Origins

The militant insistence in Defoe's prefaces to his narratives that his accounts are particular and localized histories of individuals does not mean that the form his work takes is without precedents. In *Robinson Crusoe*, Defoe purposefully cultivates scenes from famous works, some named as specific allusions and others embedded unmistakably into the narrative grid of the action. It is not strange that the story of a castaway hero would have allusive, indeed, as Defoe himself says, allegorical overtones. That seems to be the impulse of most famous stories of wanderers and survivors. When, after a twenty year absence from home, the Homeric Odysseus approaches his father he tells a story that is at once notably allegorical and, in its way, quite accurate: "I come from Rover's Passage where my home is, / and I'm King Allwoes' only son. / My name is Quarrelman."[13]

Crusoe is very much the same rover, son of woe, whose inclination, if not his name, means trouble. By his own recounting he is also the allegorical son of biblical Prodigality, the figure who wanders by design and who returns reformed. Behind the story of the prodigal son is also the archetypal story of the exiled nation; Crusoe images his plight in the figure of the Jews of Sinai and says so, admiring "the Hand of God's Providence, which had thus spread my Table in the Wilderness" (130). As rooted as he may be to the depiction of the private individual in his narratives, Defoe works with common archetypes in subtle ways. For example, no one can read the scenes of Crusoe's arrival or departure on his island without thinking of the most famous of shipwrecked mariners, Odysseus; and no one can read the complicated machinery of Crusoe's complicated rescue finale without thinking of the romance of Shakespeare's island fiction, *The Tempest*. The action at the end on Crusoe's island is a cross between an Odyssean housecleaning and a *Tempest*-like masquerade. Further, any island story, whether Homer's, Shakespeare's, or Defoe's, builds on a narrative pattern of separation, displacement, and resubstantiation so important to Western literature. The appeal of island stories has always to do with the reserves of individual resourcefulness under the most difficult of circumstances.

At the center of the famous island fictions of Western literature are notions of craft, ingenuity, and power. The control over island spaces is an almost magical motif in the *Odyssey*, *The Tempest*, and, toward its end, *Robinson Crusoe*. Islands conjure up the double image of sea and land. A mastery over both presents itself as a necessity for ocean-girted civilizations. There is an incident or, more accurately, a prophecy in the *Odyssey* that reappears in *Robinson Crusoe* in a fascinating way. Odysseus cannot be fully settled at home until he inscribes himself so widely in his wanderings that he discovers a nation that knows nothing of the sea life. The blind prophet Teiresias tells him that his oar must be planted in a fully grounded place.

> But after you have dealt out death—in open
> combat or by stealth—to all the suitors,
> go overland on foot, and take an oar,
> until one day you come where men have lived
> with meat unsalted, never known the sea,
> nor seen seagoing ships, with crimson bows
> and oars that fledge light hulls for dipping flight.
> The spot will soon be plain to you, and I
> can tell you how: some passerby will say,
> "What winnowing fan is that upon your shoulder?"

Halt, and implant your smooth oar in the turn
and make fair sacrifice to Lord Poseidon:
a ram, a bull, a great buck boar; turn back,
and carry out pure hekatombs at home
to all wide heaven's lords, the undying gods,
to each in order. Then a seaborne death
soft as this hand of mist will come upon you
when you are wearied out with rich old age,
your country folk in blessed peace around you.
And all this shall be just as I foretell.

(*Odyssey*, book II, 188–89)

In the *Odyssey* this prophecy has something to do with rooting out the lust for wandering and for adventure and instilling the desire for permanent settlement. The impulse is not altogether different from Crusoe's story where the adventurer overcomes seaborne isolation by domesticating his island territory. But Crusoe plants his oar at the beginning rather than at the end of his adventure. Having transferred the material from his wrecked ship onto a makeshift raft, Crusoe awaits a shift in offshore currents to land. He can barely hold fast and with an emphatic and symbolic gesture just manages to do so "by sticking my two broken Oars into the Ground" (52). Establishing his ground on the island, stocked with material booty, his first store, is for Crusoe an opportunity to limit the wandering inclination that he thinks causes the miseries of his "dreadful Life" (131). The essence of the island fable in Western literature is to find a way to control the impulses that initiate the trauma of separation from home. The same is true for the *Odyssey* and *The Tempest*. Planting oars on land, a grounding of the seagoing implement, is an act of well-earned settlement. Hence, Crusoe plants his oars as Odysseus will, perhaps, plant his, turned from the sea toward a "blessed" landed refuge.

All of this is to identify a shared allegiance for Defoe's *Crusoe*, not to identify a specific source for the narrative. Source study, at any rate, is a dreary pursuit for works in a genre so various and textured as the novel. Represented events in prose fiction take on a life of their own, and to identify the source of a writer's work is not necessarily to comprehend the full nature of his or her inspiration. Nonetheless, scholars try. The name of one real life mariner, Alexander Selkirk, has traditionally come down as the castaway upon whom Defoe based his *Robinson Crusoe*. Defoe well knew the circumstances of the Selkirk account, as did most everyone in London, it having been relayed fully in Woodes Rogers's *Cruising Voyage Round the World* (1712), in Edward Cooke's *Voyage to the South Sea* (1712), and in a famous account by Richard Steele in the periodical *The Englishman* (no. 26, 3 December 1713).

Much of Selkirk's story is, however, antithetical to Crusoe's. His island was not exactly in Crusoe's backyard; it was off Mas a Tierra, four hundred miles from the coast of Chile and thousands of miles from where Defoe places Crusoe in the Orinoco River basin on the opposite side of the South American continent. Moreover, Selkirk was not shipwrecked. In September 1704 he chose to stay on the isle of Juan Fernandez because of a dispute with the captain of his ship. This was a rare but not unheard of practice for disgruntled mariners. His volcanic island was fifteen miles long, heavily wooded in its northern regions, and possessed of a bay accessible to shipping lanes. Selkirk was well stocked for his four-year stay, and he would have been off his island much sooner had he not scurried to hide in caves when Spanish landing parties surveyed the island.

In February 1709, Woodes Rogers rescued Selkirk. Rogers was a privateer backed by Bristol merchants, and he had two ships and a Spanish galleon with him at the time. Selkirk was in none too good shape when discovered. Even with supplies he had turned slightly feral, lost proficiency in language, and appeared deranged. Selkirk was closer to the "meer Savage" that Crusoe imagines himself had he not transformed his island with the supplies from the shipwreck:

> Another Reflection was of great Use to me, and doubtless would
> be so to any one that should fall into such Distress as mine was;
> and this was, To compare my present Condition with what I at
> first expected it should be; nay, with what it would certainly have

been, if the good Providence of God had not wonderfully order'd the Ship to be cast up nearer to the Shore, where I not only could come at her, but could bring what I got out of her to the Shore, for my Relief and Comfort; without which, I had wanted for Tools to work, Weapons for Defence, or Gun-Powder and Shot for getting my Food. (130)

That Defoe recognized the narrative appeal of Selkirk's tale is clear; that he borrowed from it extensively in *Crusoe* is not. The experience of chasing goats, reading the Bible, making skins for clothing, and counting cats are the mainstays of what Defoe took from the Selkirk accounts. To put it another way, Defoe gleaned the marketable potential of a story such as Selkirk's, but his own strange and surprising adventures of *Robinson Crusoe* were conceived and executed on a very different basis. Defoe's imagination did not work by adapting ready-made accounts, but by ruminating after his own fashion on subjects of particular interest to him for years.

From the almost obsessive repetition of policy positions and plans in Defoe's voluminous journalism it is possible to surmise that whenever he had a story to tell it was inevitably in the descriptive service of a major project or a major grievance. Ideas about events generated and formed in his brain, and issues of abiding concern in one sphere of Defoe's life invariably got transmuted and refitted in another. *Robinson Crusoe* is no exception. Many elements of his story, especially its setting in regard to trade, "the Whore I really doated upon, and design'd to have taken up with," had nagged at him for decades.[14] He indulged this whore shamelessly when his beloved King William took power after the Glorious Revolution of 1688. Defoe began dreaming of an increase of British trading activity into the northern and southern hemispheres of the Americas. What Defoe saw as the imperial mission of a new and tolerant ruling dispensation in England was a vastly expanded program of commercial exploration.

His interest in the region where he set *Robinson Crusoe* is linked to a career-long scheme for settling targeted ports along the coasts of South America to connect that hemisphere, under the aegis of British shipping, to the West Indies and the North American trade triangle. To do so he envisioned small colonizing outposts run with the resources of native labor, the extant structure of the Spanish and Portuguese bureaucracy, and English mercantile know-how. Defoe always insisted that one English colonist was worth ten times as much to England abroad than he was at home, an observation that has relevance for the fictional enterprise of *Crusoe.*

Defoe had advocated to King William detailed plans for settling the English on the coasts of South America, boasting in his journal the *Review* how he "had the honour to lay a proposal before his late King William in the beginning of the [Spanish Succession] War" (*Defoe's Review,* 8:165). The crumbling imperial empire of Spain provided the perfect opportunity to cash in on territories and trade routes. Defoe was no mere opportunist in these matters; his thinking was global and also involved the long-range English rivalry with France over the fruits of the Spanish empire. In a tract on the partition of Spain before the outbreak of war, *The Two Great Questions Consider'd* (1700), Defoe asked a ringing series of questions on overseas trade: "What is England without its trade, without its Plantation trade, Turky and Spanish trade, and where will that be when a French garrison is planted at Cadiz, and the French fleet brings home the plate from Havana? What will the Virginia colony be worth when the French . . . have a free commerce from Quebec to Mexico behind ye?" (24).

Defoe always sought in his proposals some kind of arrangement that would enlist the best resources of the Spanish and the English against the French: the infracolonial structure of the Spanish-speaking New World and the efficiency and trade expertise of the British. He had a distrust of colonial plundering as the sole policy in the area. He was not by nature a pirate nor a plunderer; he was a trader, a maker, a manufacturer, a projector, a negotiator. And so, for the most part, is Robinson Crusoe, albeit on a fictionally limited scale, whenever he has the opportunity to deal with those, either Spanish or Portuguese, who hold power in the colonial regions in which his adventure is set.

As the War of Spanish Succession raged on during the first decade of the eighteenth century, Defoe revived his settlement proposal as part of a scheme to pay the nation's debts by founding the South Sea Company. One of England's leading ministers, Robert Harley, the man for whom Defoe worked, set up the company's charter in 1711. Defoe also advised Harley to deal for ports in the Spanish West Indies, Cuba, and even Vera Cruz, remaining convinced that King William would have tried to effect these ventures had he lived.

Defoe's discrete points of desire, the places that made his colonial mouth water, were on the Chilean coast and in the area around Guiana, the latter being the area of Crusoe's settlement near the "Draft and Reflux of the mighty River *Oroonooko*" (215). The Orinoco basin is important to Defoe and to *Robinson Crusoe* for other reasons. England's legendary colonizing adventurer, the great Sir Walter Raleigh, had centered his hopes for the city of gold, El Dorado, in this same river basin. Defoe's story is thus set in territory that had already achieved a mythic dimension for British exploration. Moreover, Raleigh's dream had come to symbolize for Defoe his own obsession with commercial expansion. Raleigh was a man with a sovereign vision and a personal doggedness in the name of English colonization. On the human scale Raleigh was all dash, like that wonderful "amphibean" creature Defoe describes in *Moll Flanders* as a gentleman tradesman; on the mercantile scale Raleigh was all risk, adventure, and discovery, behavior dear to Defoe's heart. Defoe may even have thought, according to some of his biographers, that his family was distantly related to Raleigh's and that the blood of that Renaissance merchant adventurer flowed through his own veins.

Though the case is somewhat disputed, Defoe probably had a hand in writing *A Historical Account of Sir Walter Raleigh* (1720). There is a passage in that work where the author recalls Defoe's interest in the region of the Orinoco, including a plan to lay before the South Sea Company in 1719, the year of *Crusoe*'s publication: "[He] lay before them a plan or chart of the rivers and shores, the depths of the water, and all necessary instructions for the navigation, with a scheme of the undertaking, which he had the honour about thirty years ago to lay before King William, and to demonstrate how easy it would be to bring the attempt to perfection" (55).

It was the resumption of war with Spain in that year, 1719, that refocused Defoe's attention. He knew that England would be ill served by simply ravaging Spanish coastal holdings, though he had schemed for private buccaneers to probe into Spain's most vulnerable ports. His position when he wrote *Crusoe* was subtler. He wished for England to be, as would be Crusoe in his dealings, tactically amicable towards Spain and Portugal, looking for gaps in the areas of imperial control, proposing English inroads in coastal areas where there would be neither the will nor the interest to oppose them.

With all this as a background to *Crusoe,* it is hardly surprising when two months before the publication of his novel, Defoe wrote about the Orinoco basin in the *Weekly Journal,* 7 February 1719:

> We expect, in two or three Days, a most flaming Proposal from the South Sea Company, or from a Body of Merchants who claim kindred of them, for erecting a British Colony on the Foundation of the South-Sea Company's Charter, upon the Terra Firma, or the Northernmost Side of the Mouth of the great River Oroonoko. They propose, as we hear, the establishing a Factory and Settlement there, which shall cost the Company 500000£. Sterling. . . . This, it seems, is the same Country and River discovered by Sir Walter Rawleigh, in former Days, and that which he miscarried in by several Mistakes, which may now easily be prevented.

Much in *Robinson Crusoe* gains its shape from Defoe's legitimate river basin prospectus scaled down to an island pipe dream.[15] The reformative struggle with the coastal natives on and off the island at the end of the fable, Crusoe's sense of fair-minded Spanish and Portuguese, and, finally, his despair at the behavior of the English on his island illustrate Defoe's concerns about colonialism. At the end Crusoe gains what colonial solace he has lost thinking about his own countrymen from his man Friday's thinking about his. Friday promises to reform his countrymen, the cannibals on the South American main, because *"they willing love learn"* (225). He means by this that they would be willing to learn and would love doing so, no small measure of relief to Crusoe. Friday expresses his utopian vision of colonial life when Crusoe tests him about whether to join him on a boat voyage to the main: *"You do great deal much good,* says he, *you teach wild Mans be good sober tame Mans; you tell them know God, pray God, and live new Life"* (226). It is interesting that Crusoe would have taught Friday words such as "sober" and "tame." Words make the man and, in this sense, make the labor pool. Sober, tame men do not as a rule eat potential European colonizers or, more to the point, do not eat Crusoe. Crusoe thus settles into his potential in regard to Friday and his people: "Upon the whole, as I found by all his Discourse a settled Affection to me, and that nothing should part him from me, so I found all the Foundation of his Desire to go to his own Country, was laid in his ardent Affection to the People, and his Hopes of my doing them good" (227).

Defoe plays many colonial angles in the last part of Crusoe's adventures. There is a future possible on the main, a cooperative one. When the cannibals come ashore with European prisoners, Crusoe releases a bound and exhausted white man, who says in Latin *"Christianus"* (235). That is the first word from a European he has heard in twenty-seven years, and it announces a European allegiance and a colonial policy. The man is Spanish and Christian, though Catholic; the English Protestant, Crusoe, arms him, and they join to kill some natives, who are defenseless on the beach, before scheming to ally with natives on the main.

Crusoe directly asks the Spaniard whether an alliance is possible between himself and the Spanish already befriended by other mainland cannibals. Though Crusoe has in mind saving his own skin, the question he asks is the same Defoe asked for over three decades in a more general sense. Is there the possibility of cooperation between the English and the Spanish in colonizing the coastal territories of the region? He wants to strike a kind of client deal. The Spaniard gives Crusoe an answer about his countrymen that Defoe hopes might serve history: "they would abhor the Thought of using any Man unkindly that should contribute to their Deliverance" in that "they were all of them very civil honest Men" (245). Defoe writes this at a time when England and Spain are at war in 1719, and he risks the ire of his countrymen to court an expanded colonial policy. That was his way.

The English mutineers who next show up on the island are much less interested in settlement opportunities than the Spanish who are already in cahoots with the natives. Indeed, the English who remain on the island for the second part of Crusoe's adventures are an ornery and troublesome lot. English action in the area is unreliable; the Spaniards are the source of an effective new order. When Crusoe does get off his island and begins ferreting out his finances from his plantation holdings in Brazil he finds the Portuguese have the same sense of things as the Spanish. Some of the earnings from his plantation cannot be recovered because the finances have been administered, on the one hand, for church charity and, on the other, for state power. The Procurator Fiscal has spent Crusoe's money largely to convert the natives of the region, a program motivated not merely by religious good feeling but by the economic benefits of a loyal colonized labor force.

By the time Defoe was writing and preparing the sequel to *Crusoe, The Farther Adventures*, he had fairly much lost hope in his schemes. Defoe's great mercantile dream, like Raleigh's El Dorado, had few takers at home. And by 1720 the disastrous collapse of all South Sea ventures with the crash of stock shares known as the South Sea Bubble made colonization untenable. Though a good part of the *Crusoe* sequel is taken up with what happens to Crusoe's settlement, the island is essentially unfantasized and badly colonized. The region's moment has passed by. Crusoe returns to his island after a hiatus of nine years to set his squabbling colonists aright. But despite his civic-mindedness, no real colony ever gets going amid the domestic discord, small-mindedness, and ill-spiritedness of island life. Crusoe ends up doctrinaire in all the areas where he is innovative in the original. Having done it all his way, he thinks everyone else on the island should do so as well. Earlier in the adventure he let the parrot who always called his name free, and he points out that "perhaps poor Poll may be alive there still, calling after *Poor Robin Crusoe* to this Day" (180). There is something sad about this. Colonists settle after Crusoe is gone and befoul his island estate. But there is still a plaintive voice on the island that announces his presence. This may be the proprietary price of imperial dreams and their reality as well.

Having set Crusoe in the Orinoco River basin and having tried to explain why, Defoe touches on another subject that concerned him all his life: the nature of individual sovereignty and the politics of island life. Crusoe spends twenty-eight years castaway on his island. The dates are carefully plotted. He lands in September 1659, and he returns to England in June 1687, a fold of years that virtually overlaps the first twenty-eight years of Defoe's life as well as the twenty-eight-year period in England toward which Defoe directed a lifelong antagonism, the Restoration of the Stuart kings from 1660 to 1688. That Crusoe leaves just before the Stuarts return and returns just before they leave is a coincidence far too powerful to ignore.

It may seem as if by 1719 the experience of the Restoration monarchy is wearing historically thin as a subject demanding Defoe's attention. But Defoe's challenge in *Crusoe* is to rewrite the obsessions of a lifetime into the story of a life. For Defoe the Restoration was a watershed experience in England, one in which he himself engaged in radical and dangerous activities to hasten the departure of the Stuarts. Over and again in his writings Defoe referred to the 1688 Glorious Revolution that rid England of the Stuarts as a personal and national rebirth, the dawning of an age of entrepreneurial energy and political toleration.

Crusoe's time on his island is a counterreign of sorts. As an island king he is a native exile. In a variation of the classical exile story, Crusoe symbolically holds his land's values in trust until the time is ripe for return. As so many readers have intuited, Crusoe stands for something central in the English experience, and for Defoe to hold him in place for twenty-eight years during a critical phase of English history is to make a telling point about the survival of national values in the face of what he saw as political recidivism.

In setting the time scheme of *Crusoe* to play out an implicit undercurrent of national values, Defoe is not writing in a vacuum. When he claims that the fable of Crusoe is comparable to "the historical parables in the Holy Scripture, such 'The Pilgrim's Progress,' and such, in a word, the adventures of your fugitive friend, 'Robinson Crusoe' " (*Works*, 3: 107), he writes in a way consistent with narrative practice in Protestant Europe. In a revealing chapter titled "Moral Geography" from his book on the Dutch, *The Embarrassment of Riches: An Interpretation of Dutch Culture in the Golden Age,* Simon Schama speaks of a fully developed genre, in woodcuts, prints, legends, and narrative accounts, that he calls the "survival ordeal." The survival ordeal was "targeted at an audience that expected good fortune to be struck by retributive calamity from which only the virtuous and heroic might escape."[16] Schama's description of the Dutch genre parallels aspects of Defoe's project in *Crusoe.* The scene or story usually represents "ships in remote or terrifying circumstances, trapped in Arctic ice or battered by tropical storms, and of fights with horribly tattooed savages" (Schama, 28).

What makes the survival ordeal remarkable for the Protestant Dutch is the overlay with providential or saving remnant narratives, where grace is accorded to the rigorous and pious in the face of severe political trials. The American Puritan experience—the Pilgrim story being a prominent instance—is rife with similar narrative accounts of chosen remnants, spiritually select and materially tough folk who replay the basic patterns of biblical exilic or outcast history in their new, or newly won, lands. To place the issue in a wider context, Schama seems to understand the implicit political message in the national addiction to saving remnant narratives, a message that is central in the establishment of what he calls the citizen hero in distinction to the aristocratic or honor-based hero of the monarchical European state. He writes about the revolutionary Dutch, but the same holds for the Puritans in America or the radical Protestant forces in England so opposed, as was Defoe, to the ruling principles of the Stuart kings: "Part of this addiction was the perennial fascination with danger, lived vicariously, and the need for citizen-heroes in a young republic that had repudiated the imperial aura of the Hapsburgs" (Schama, 30).

During the seventeenth century, the Protestant Dutch cast their lot on what Schama calls the "great historical ocean" (30) of trade when that nation of citizen heroes survived and, indeed, thrived apart from their Spanish masters. Defoe had special reason to key into this sort of thinking about the national values of narrative action during a period of comparable historical shifts in England, at least from his point of view. He was born into a dissenting family, and he was spiritually and politically akin to those who had left Stuart England to settle in America and to those whose politics at home, in varying degrees of radicalism, had shaped the civil wars of the mid-seventeenth century.

To be born in the very year of a returned Stuart monarchy made the notion of a saving or surviving remnant narrative especially poignant for Defoe and facilitated the principle manifest in *Crusoe* of an individual life as nationally symbolic. Like Defoe during the Restoration, Crusoe is a twenty-eight-year survivor; he lasts it out on his island until the time is ready for him to go home. The length of Crusoe's exile may seem secondary to Crusoe's survival on his island, but it is really instrumental to it. He lives completely apart from what Defoe considered the dynastic blemish of Stuart rule and represents a different vision of the course of English history, a vision that counts on substituting citizen-based values for monarchical ones, material individualism for absolute rule, and toleration for religious persecution. These shifts in policy after 1688 were to set the course for England for the next several hundred years.

On his island Crusoe makes numerous references to himself as king, references that get at the gist of the story as a political fable. Defoe is characteristically witty in his references to island rule, but that is part of his point. Kingship is mere posturing without legal, ethical, moral principles to balance its impulses. Here, for example, is Crusoe toward the end of his stay when his island begins to test his powers of rule:

> My island was now peopled, and I thought my self very rich in Subjects; and it was a merry Reflection which I frequently made, How like a King I look'd. First of all, the whole Country was my own meer Property; so that I had an undoubted Right of Dominion. 2*dly*, My People were perfectly subjected: I was absolute Lord and Law-giver; they all owed their Lives to me, and were ready to lay down their Lives, *if there had been Occasion of it*, for me. It was remarkable too, we had but three Subjects, and they were of three different Religions. My Man *Friday* was a Protestant, his Father was a *Pagan* and a *Cannibal*, and the *Spaniard* was a Papist: However, I allow'd Liberty of Conscience throughout my Dominions: But this is by the Way. (241)

Crusoe can afford to joke because the notion of diadem here is inherently funny and the royal "we" a studied affectation. Better yet is the doublet, "*Pagan* and a *Cannibal*," a pairing at once descriptively accurate and religiously bizarre. But there is a serious side to Crusoe's banter. The whole of the book has been about the personal meaning of sovereignty, set during those years when the issues of legitimacy, absolutism, toleration, and rights were paramount in any Englishman's notion of human affairs. Dressed as he is, and controlling what he does, Crusoe may appear ludicrous as a king, but it is no accident that his mock-political program is one of extended toleration. Defoe always advocated such a program for England; it was one that ushered in the reign of his much-loved William III and one that at very best the Stuarts before William cynically mangled and manipulated for political advantage.

Defoe's own radical activity against the Stuarts in the late 1670s and early 1680s arose out of his conviction that these kings were absolutists and dynastic tyrants at heart. He suspected their politics, their motives, and their policies in regard to personal liberties and national interests. In an early issue of his *Review* in 1704 he reflects on an ill-starred attempt by radicals to assassinate the second Stuart king, Charles I, commenting on the madness of the scheme but wondering enigmatically, "what should we have call'd it, if it had succeeded?" (*Defoe's Review*, 10 June 1704, 1:127). The answer is implicitly tyrannicide, an action that has its defenders among people for whom Defoe had implicit respect. Defoe's twelve-book poem, *Jure Divino* (1706), which charts the full case against the Stuarts and reveals the intricacies of his position on the exercise, correct and abusive, of monarchical power, essentially says about the Stuarts what Rousseau said years later: "the spirit of injustice and tyranny in them was their dominant characteristic."[17]

Whatever the whimsy of Crusoe's reign, it reflects one overriding concern of Defoe's, a concern that complemented the range of his interests and effectively linked his intellectual life to his politics. Crusoe manages in his latter days on the island to substitute toleration for tyranny. For Defoe, toleration is the best indication of social and mental health. He valued the principle as the Enlightenment philosophers were to value it after him and as the founders of the American Constitution were to value it later in the century. Only a tolerant state is a truly productive one. Defoe's critique of tryanny is always a defense of toleration, which encourages the inclusion of all groups in society who contribute to the political and economic welfare of the nation. When Defoe took positions on politics he did so in the name of inclusion, where the notion of a society run by tyrannous preserves of state power, by court favorites, by political spoils gives way to a moderate and systemic spirit of sane, legal, tolerant, rational sovereign power.

For Defoe it is Crusoe on his island who sustains values that are purposeful and national. Defoe makes the same point dramatically and directly in his *Journal of the Plague Year* (1722) when, during the height of the Restoration's 1665 Bubonic Plague, he has the much abused English Dissenters, barred by the five-mile act to the outskirts of London, actually take over the city's parish churches, from which they were banned by law, to serve the sick. They do so because the Stuart pensioners and Anglican officials have absconded to the country. Civic responsibility is a matter of conscience as well as interest, and those who act best are the state's best representatives no matter what their rights or where they live, be it outside the city walls of London, in America, or on island in the Orinoco River basin.

Toleration has the same resonance as liberty, another principle that embodies an intellectual sense of expansion and a social or political sense of variety represented in *Robinson Crusoe*. Defoe would always poise toleration and liberty over their nefarious counterprinciples, qualification and tyranny. Having Crusoe, a free man on his island, substitute for the Stuart Restoration is a potent private message in Defoe's narrative. Toleration and liberty are the sine qua non of sensible life. They are marks of character in individuals and in states.

Even, or especially, in island isolation Crusoe has to battle with himself over the principle of toleration and come out a winner to govern his island properly. In the interim between Crusoe's thoughts about redirecting his efforts toward home and his opportunity to make the break, he begins to revise his notions of what political and national life ought to mean to him. With his intuition of deliverance, he turns in his thinking from violent retribution against the cannibals to the law of tolerant nations. And he does so by readjusting his view of those whose presence on his side of the island had long ago so reduced him to quivering paranoia and unaccountable bloodlust.

God has not called on him, Crusoe says, "to take upon me to be a Judge of their Actions, much less an Executioner of his Justice; that whenever he thought fit, he would take the Cause into his own Hands, and by national Vengeance punish them as a People, for nationalist Crimes; but that in the mean time, it was none of my Business" (232). Any one individual or any constituted sovereign power cannot establish legitimacy on principles deriving solely from cultural or religious difference. Such policies always sow the seeds of violence.

Despite his views on toleration and liberty expressed through Crusoe on his island, Defoe was not a classical republican. He had his doubts about the notion of a common governmental voice even though he believed in common interests. Rather, he honored the possibility of rational monarchical government because he believed in the necessity of a central vision, of the emanation of power from an authority with enforcing energies. But he did not believe power was mystical—that is divinely granted—nor that it came without severe limitations and obligations. He was revolutionary against the abuse of power when he had to be, though he was not revolutionary for the mere thrill of it. He welcomed the principle of the lawful king, but he took the principle literally; law and kingship must justify rather than excuse one another.

The notion of island rule and the political ideas that surface in *Crusoe* gain credence near the end of the island narrative when shiploads of different people, from cannibals to mutineers, begin to vie for island power. At one point, Crusoe chooses to ally himself with the rightful captain of a ship whose crew has dispossessed him. This seems almost a miniature version of the story of island legitimacy that has controlled the political structure of the entire narrative. As the rightful captain of the English vessel looks at the bizarre figure coming toward him, Crusoe plays the mythical stranger-savior figure of legendary tales. He says to the captain: "But can you put a Stranger in the way how to help you, for you seem to me to be in some great Distress? I saw you when you landed, and when you seem'd to make Applications to the Brutes that came with you, I saw one of them lift up his Sword to kill you" (254).

The English captain wonders, *"Am I talking to God or Man! Is it a real Man, or an Angel!"* (254). Crusoe's self-identification is revealing: "I am a Man, an *Englishman,* and dispos'd to assist you" (254–55). Once an island sovereign, Crusoe now names himself citizen of his native land. In the name of legitimacy, he takes on national origin. When he returns to the civilized world he does so perfectly restored: "It is impossible to express here the Flutterings of my very Heart, when I look'd over these Letters, and especially when I found all my Wealth about me" (284). Wealth and stuff are the store or future laid in against life's exigencies. This is the point that Defoe makes as strongly as an Englishman could by placing Crusoe on the island during the historical Restoration only to restore him at home when that period ends: "I was now Master, all on a Sudden, of above 5000 £. *Sterling* in Money, and had an Estate, as I might well call it, in the *Brasils,* of above a thousand Pounds a Year, as sure as an Estate of Lands in *England:* And in a Word, I was in a Condition which I scarce knew how to understand, or how to compose my self, for the Enjoyment of it" (285). His accumulated property allows him to return, in a sense, properly islanded. Perhaps in a still broader sense, Crusoe's return to his native country allows Defoe to realize the full potential of a narrative form in which the saving remnant is always sovereign.

By combining his life-long colonial interests in the region of the Crusoe fable with his pointed dating game in placing Crusoe out of England and on his island for the bulk of the Stuart Restoration, Defoe collapses the historical past into the historical future. He sustains in Crusoe the national mission, the hoped for westward course of British empire, by having him represent in his island reign the settlement ethos over and beyond the absolutist ethos of home rule. He is the English spirit of merchant adventure awaiting opportunity by making something substantial of the time given him. In the Crusoe fable, England literally comes out from under Stuart hegemony to test her future sea legs in the arena of world commerce. That Defoe was thinking somewhat along these lines becomes clear in the *Farther Adventures* when Crusoe's extended travels as merchant adventurer take him to many of the world's major trading outposts. He is the new man for an age who, like Defoe, begins by waiting out the old order and ends by inscribing the world for his merchant wanderlust. This is precisely the way James Joyce read Defoe's *Crusoe*, a book he called the English *Ulysses* when he characterized it as the "prophecy of empire" and Robinson Crusoe as the "true symbol of the British conquest" (*Buffalo Studies*, 24).

6

The Psychology of Everyday Island Life

Robinson Crusoe provides an early and intense instance of what literary historian Ian Watt long ago identified as the central subject in the new fiction of the early eighteenth century, the realistic configuration of a life in a circumstantially recognizable place. Defoe's novel is a story of the way material space and physical things reflect the drives, the fantasies, the fetishes of the individual. Why does Crusoe act as he does? What motivates him? Why does he hoard and stockpile, almost on reflex? Where do his violent urgings come from? It is not just what Crusoe manipulates and arranges on his island that make him what he is in the fiction but what impresses him, how his mind disposes of the things he sees and thinks about. Crusoe's field of vision combines things sighted, touched, arranged, and known with mental impressions, with apprehensions, anxieties, fevers, and dreams. Defoe has imagined an island mentality and called it, after a fashion, *Crusoe.*

If island space is in many ways the map of Crusoe's mind, there are two sorts of spatial metaphors in the narrative that translate into psychological states. One is expansive and aggrandizing—Crusoe opening up the island, increasing his store and storage, exploring new territory. The other is protective and enclosing—Crusoe closing off things, secreting, hiding, camouflaging. On the one hand he cultivates and landscapes, and on the other he divides his store into ever smaller components within caves, circles of stakes within circles of stakes. For most of the island stay those two impulses, expansive and protective, mark Crusoe's sense of space as they mark his sense of life. Crusoe will take ludicrous chances in some instances, whereas he is cautious to a fault in others.

The fantasy structure of *Crusoe* is dependent not only on the construct of an island space onto which Crusoe imposes his double sovereignty, open and hidden, but on the way he materializes experience, on the way he accumulates, builds, arranges, and stores. Life for Crusoe is a kind of exercise in material possession and possessiveness. Defoe understood such a notion as a basic psychological idea, though in modern times Freud has gone much further in addressing the relation of the inner self to the outside world, of the things one produces to the things one owns or has. Stuff in all forms is a kind of bodily extension. Perhaps because Crusoe reveals so much about his spaces and his possessions he feels less need to detail the exigencies of bodily life that so occupy a satirist's view, say, Swift's of Crusoe's rival traveler and castaway, Lemuel Gulliver. Swift makes what might literally be called a huge issue of Gulliver's body right from the beginning, including habits of hygiene and defecation. In contrast, Crusoe has built everything on the island except a natural sewer system or a cesspool.

But Defoe's realism produces another kind of bodily awareness, one produced by the power of psychological obsession. Just how much, for example, do readers have to know about the ever increasing and thickening and secretly entwined rows of trees that hide Crusoe's domestic habitat to begin to think, as Crusoe does himself, about his fear of exposure and penetration? Or just how far do readers have to trace the recurring cannibal theme in the narrative to guess, as does the critic Everett Zimmerman, that Crusoe fixates on being eaten alive? There is sufficient reason for fear in a strange and alien place, but Crusoe goes further—he makes caution into necessity.

Given his strong compulsion to protect and camouflage, all his desirable island spots—his town and country houses, his seaside estates—are transformable into other things: caves, fortresses, defense perimeters. And all can recede back into the perfectly natural.

Defoe tends to work with motifs in his fiction that take on incremental value as his stories progress. Narrative takes up the consciousness of character, reflects in the way a character thinks and speaks the obsessions that rule his or her psyche. In *Moll Flanders*, for example, Defoe builds on the motif of impulse for both Moll's sexual adventures and her criminal ones. In *Roxana*, he builds on the motif of discovery. *Robinson Crusoe* works and reworks the motif of conversion. Conversion is at the heart of the narrative. To set a man on an empty island means that everything has to be converted to Crusoe's use to have significance; hence the novel is in a direct and metaphoric sense about varieties of conversion: fear to salvation; stuff to structure; nature to culture; accident to providence; paranoia to toleration. Crusoe makes over his island, turns his religious sensibility, shifts his politics, transforms his life. Turning things around or seeing another side—to see the other side of the island actually becomes one of Crusoe's obsessions—is what Crusoe does and what makes him who he is.

When Crusoe arrives on his island the place is already a haven from the sea, "the comfortable Part of my Condition" (47), though a threat from inland, "neither did I see any Prospect before me, but that of perishing with Hunger, or being devour'd by wild Beasts" (47). It is this double condition that he works to transform on the island—he would make his refuge less of a potential threat and more a secure home. Little by little, bit by bit, Crusoe makes over the island, converts it into a habitable estate.

The challenge for Crusoe is to widen the circle around him in which he feels "the comfortable Part of my Condition." Defoe sets this up deliberately, first having Crusoe crawl "up into a thick bushy Tree" (47) for protection during his first night on the island; then,

Crusoe's island shipwreck.
From Robinson Crusoe *(London: Cassell, Petter & Galpin, 1869).*

after removing material the next day from the wreck, setting up Crusoe and his possessions in a kind of enclave that miniaturizes what will be his later relation with the island at large: "I barricado'd my self round with the Chests and Boards that I had brought on Shore" (53). As he increases his store from the ship, he changes his nomenclature and expands his domain: "I was gotten home to my little Tent, where I lay with all my Wealth about me very secure" (57).

The subtle naming of self surrounded by property as home is part of the intricate psychologizing of island space that takes place in the narrative. Defoe holds to the notion that provision is part of one's providence. It is not in God's plan to have all things stay the same. The material world is at one's disposal. To be a better person is to make use of material as well as spiritual opportunity. Defoe articulates this notion in an essay, *Mere Nature Delineated* (1726), in which he has occasion to write on Peter the Wild Boy of Germany. The position he takes in that work, as Maximillian Novak has argued, throws important light on *Crusoe*. Essentially, Defoe claims that the nature of man resides in his capacity for improvement in the context of a material world. That is, nature is not a state that necessarily produces its own progress. Man is better for the learned institutional values inculcated by religion, by political systems, by education, by information, by technical science, by law. In this sense, it is not the state of nature that makes Crusoe what he is and the island experience what it is, but the remnants of the material world from which Crusoe comes. He does himself over better by living with the assistance of civilization's provisions from the wrecked ship.

Crusoe surrounded by all his stuff from the wreck makes himself at home on the island in ways he might never have been able to do anywhere else; and that is precisely because making himself at home is not a luxury but a necessity. His character improves as he sets the relation between self and property. The process does not end with the tent, for it occurs to Crusoe soon enough that he can expand yet again by adapting to his topography, finding a little plain on a hill whose "Front towards this little Plain, was steep as a House-side" (58). He stakes out a half circle on the plain around an indentation in the hillside and insulates himself again—Crusoe and his property are again islanded: "The Entrance into this Place I made to be not by a Door, but by a short Ladder to go over the Top, which Ladder, when I was in, I lifted over after me, and so I was compleatly fenc'd in, and fortify'd, as I thought, from all the World, and consequently slept secure in the Night" (59).

Needless to say, Crusoe understands what has become a reflex. Having expanded his domicile, he sleeps with his property. This is the founding action of the new family circle. The image is both complex and comforting, obsessive and protective, fencing and for-tifying, all things that make Crusoe secure and happy: "Into this Fence or Fortress, with infinite Labour, I carry'd all my Riches, all my Provisions, Ammunition and Stores, of which you have the Account above, and I made me a large Tent, which to preserve me from the Rains that in one Part of the Year are very violent there, I made double, *viz.* One smaller Tent within, and one larger Tarpaulin which I had sav'd among the Sails" (59–60).

He further expands by digging into the rock, which "serv'd me like a Cellar to my House" (60)—that is, until he begins filling it with parcels of gun powder so that it looks like his island store and "which in my Fancy I call'd my Kitchin" (61). Then the secretive nature of Crusoe kicks in. This is what makes the narrative so compelling—the island is always a natural preserve even as it becomes Crusoe's domicile, his store, his estate, his kingdom. Crusoe makes over the remote and wild exilic locale into his place, his home, but preserves its secrecy for his protection. The material design for living that Crusoe projects on his island partakes of the perfect fantasy: comfort and camouflage. He works on undoing the obvious by naturalizing his fence: "When this Wall was finished, and the Outside double fenc'd with a Turf-Wall rais'd up close to it, I perswaded my self, that if any People were to come on Shore there, they would not perceive any Thing like a Habitation" (76). He must have cannibals in mind, for it is not certain at this point that should Europeans appear he would so readily wish to disappear into the landscape.

Crusoe repeats the process of settlement, construction, and camouflage when he builds his second house on the much more beautiful inland plain after his reconnoitering of the island. His language betrays both his Europeanization of the island and his native insecurity: "I built me a little kind of a Bower, and surrounded it at a Distance with a strong Fence, being a double Hedge, as high as I could reach, well stak'd, and fill'd between with *Brushwood;* and here I lay very secure, sometimes two or three Nights together, always going over it with a Ladder, as before; so that I fancy'd now I had my Country-House, and my Sea-Coast House" (101–2).

An important process has already taken place on Crusoe's island, one that very subtly replicates the initial feeling of displacement when he first landed, but resituates that displacement not from the greater world to desert island but from his original seaside island habitation to his new habitation on the inland savanna: "I confess this Side of the Country was much pleasanter than mine, but yet I had not the least Inclination to remove; for as I was fix'd in my Habitation, it became natural to me, and I seem'd all the while I was here, to be as it were upon a Journey, and from Home" (110). The two Crusoes, the one with the wandering inclination and the other with the penchant for secure insulation, meet on the island savanna, and now, the Wandering Crusoe, having already experienced the trials of a castaway, confronts the Homebody Crusoe. The initial pattern of the book's thematic action reverses: the Homebody Crusoe wins the day this time—at least for a while.

Crusoe's pattern in his life before was to abandon what he had in anticipation of what he wanted. Now on the island he expands concentrically. He keeps his home base, precisely what he did not do earlier. The jigsawlike buildup of Crusoe's various island habitats determines much of the action in the book, and Defoe works it all very carefully up to a long summary just prior to Crusoe's famous discovery of the footprint, which epitomizes the best and worst of his desires, the possible reunion with one of his own species and the frightening thought of the penetration of his body and his domain, the two having become something of the same by this point in the action. These summary paragraphs are tactically placed because Defoe, in effect, recreates the complete spatial culture of the island at the very moment Crusoe becomes traumatized about his territory being trampled upon and penetrated by another. I cite the first sentences of a consecutive sequence of much longer paragraphs:

> You are to understand, that now I had, as I may call it, two Plantations in the Island; one my little Fortification or Tent, with the wall about it under the rock, with the Cave behind me, which by this Time I had enlarg'd into several Apartments, or Caves, one within another. . . .

As for my Wall made, *as before,* with long Stakes or Piles, those Piles grew tall like Trees. . . .

Near this Dwelling of mine, but a little farther within the Land, and upon lower Ground, lay my two Pieces of Corn-Ground. . . .

Besides this, I had my Country Seat, and I had now a tollerable Plantation there also. . . .

Adjoyning to this I had my Enclosures for my Cattle, that is to say, my Goats. . . .

In this Place also I had my Grapes growing. . . .

As this was also about half Way between my other Habitation, and the Place where I had laid up my Boat, I generally stay'd, and lay here in my Way thither. (151–53)

Here is an eighteenth-century prospect, a full factoring of a man's estates, an articulated domain. Only at this point does Defoe literally insert the most dramatic sentence of the island adventures: "It happen'd one Day about Noon going towards my Boat, I was exceedingly surpriz'd with the Print of a Man's naked Foot on the Shore" (153). This startling incursion is perhaps the most memorable event in the entire narrative. From his very first adventures, Crusoe has been obsessed with his relation to what he calls "humane Society." On a number of occasions he comments on his longing for his fellowman, but, to better effect, Defoe works the realistic details of the fiction to make a different point about Crusoe's desires. Crusoe is as apprehensive about human incursion into his new island spaces as he is desirous of it. His experiences have placed him at the margins of civilization and at the margins of civilized behavior. He has been abducted by pirates and fears being eaten by cannibals. Man is a threat as much as a promise.

Defoe builds to the famous footprint scene in a way that exhibits all the resources of the new mode of fiction that he develops. The mark in the sand is not the first foot readers have confronted. It is part of an intricate texture of fictional repetition. Much earlier, when Crusoe's first sea voyage ended in disaster at Yarmouth, his friend's seaman father told him he would "not set my Foot in the same Ship with thee again for a Thousand Pounds" (15). In the economy of

Defoe's fictional language, who puts one's foot where is a matter of utmost significance. During Crusoe's first adventure, when he escaped from the Moor with the boy, Xury, he landed on the African coast near the latitude of the Canary islands. His fear at the time was to be beset by savages, but he rests content upon spotting their landfall because Xury had seen "no wild Mans" (26) and "no Foot-steps of any humane Creature in that part of the Country" (26). This scene and this phrase are of limited significance here; they only gain importance later when Crusoe's entire demeanor, his fear, his caution, his obsession, relates to his anxiety about having another being put a mark on his space, to imprint it, to annihilate his special relation to comfort and safety.

There is another moment, again insignificant in itself, but powerful in conjunction with the way Defoe identifies Crusoe's relation to fellowmen by where they might set their feet. Here is the scene just at the moment Crusoe has been cast ashore on his island: "I walk'd about on the Shore, lifting up my Hands, and my whole Being, as I may say, wrapt up in the Contemplation of my Deliverance, making a Thousand Gestures and Motions which I cannot describe, reflecting upon all my Comrades that were drown'd, and that there should not be one Soul sav'd but my self; for, as for them, I never saw them afterwards, or any Sign of them, except three of their Hats, one Cap, and two Shoes that were not Fellows" (46).

Not one soul is saved but Crusoe. Defoe manages to convey Crusoe's despair in a few bobbing images, the last of which—"two Shoes that were not Fellows"—is extraordinary. The shoes were mismatched, but the phrasing suggests what Crusoe at that point most fears. The shoes have no feet in them to make a print—they were not *his* fellows. His gesture of despair, walking distractedly about on the shore, is ironically the same he exhibits years later when he encounters the footprint in the sand and a possible soul saved from somewhere: "I went up the Shore and down the Shore" (154).

There is a kind of fictional shadowing or ghosting of these two scenes on the beach. In the first, Crusoe feels his isolation; in the second, he fears his penetration. The linkup becomes even clearer when Crusoe reconstructs the moment in his journal entry for 30 September, the day of his first setting "Foot upon this horrid Island" (63). The mark of distinction is always a foot, which here and later, for different reasons, punctuates Crusoe's island stay: first his foot and then another's. It is fitting that at the very end of his adventure Crusoe gathers all those loose particles of clothing that had earlier symbolized for him the loss of human society. The captain of the rescue ship fits Crusoe out in a manner comporting with the civilized Englishman he claims to be. Crusoe is restored with a surplus of six shirts, "neckcloaths," gloves, shoes, hat, stockings, suit—"In a Word, he cloathed me from Head to Foot" (274).

Feet are not the only partitive symbol of human society for Crusoe that foreshadow the later scenes of island penetration. Defoe also plays, as did the master of island fiction before him, William Shakespeare in *The Tempest,* with voices. Crusoe has been on his island six years when he tries sailing around it in a canoe he had crafted. He is pulled away by the tides and reproaches himself that he had ever "repin'd at my solitary Condition; and now what would I give to be on Shore there again" (139). He manages to rebeach and, exhausted, travels to his bower, pulling his ladder over behind him, where he collapses in the shade. At this time he was "wak'd out of my Sleep by a Voice calling me by my Name several times, *Robin, Robin, Robin Crusoe,* poor *Robin Crusoe,* where are you *Robin Crusoe?* Where are you? Where have you been?" (142).

Drowsily, Crusoe thinks he dreams "some Body spoke to me," but soon wakes thoroughly and, like the subsequent footprint scene, "was at first dreadfully frighted" (142). On this occasion, he figures out to whom the other presence belongs. It is Poll the parrot, whose voice was a mimicry of Crusoe's earlier laments about his island life. The first word, however, Crusoe taught Poll was its own name. So Poll is at once its own self and a sounding of Crusoe's former self.

Crusoe had said the bird's name over and over again to get it to sound it out on its own; and the bird listened to Crusoe's name over and over again so that it could later surprise the castaway at his own business in his own voice.

By confronting this voice Crusoe confronts his own island history, his initial despair and, after identifying the parrot as the source, his present relief. The scene does take place, after all, hard upon a second island beachhead, this time back to his "beloved Island" rather than his initial *"horrible desolate Island"* (66). He feels good to be home. Moreover, Crusoe's condition in isolation is such that all his extensions of self, property or parrot, are versions of himself. He hears his name and soon is comforted, happy to be back on his island, and happier yet that his other self, even his former self in Poll, can greet him "just as if he had been overjoy'd to see me again; and so I carry'd him Home along with me" (143).

It is this reflexive quality of the self in the other that so stymies Crusoe during the footprint scene nine years later. Wandering over familiar territory, Crusoe comes upon one single large print in the sand. The paradox of his condition is immediate: the strength of character that has made him whole in isolation has distorted his social instinct. He only feels comfortable now with himself or with another, like Poll, who echoes himself. He can offer no satisfactory explanation for the appearance of the print; surely none so comforting as for the sound of the parrot.

The "Print of a Man's naked Foot on the Shore" (153) leaves Crusoe thunderstruck. It is "as if I had seen an Apparition" (153). He wants his island to fold around him, protect him: "like a Man perfectly confus'd and out of my self, I came Home to my Fortification, not feeling, as we say, the Ground I went on" (154). Out of himself he is a kind of double, self-threatening, like the apparition he thinks he has seen. But that ghost has a tangible quality; it makes a real impression on Crusoe and a real impression on the sand, whereas Crusoe is so scared his tracks are metaphorically ungrounded.

Not having made the print he approaches, he makes no tracks in retreat.

Crusoe's confusion derives from the strength of his desire that his settlement, once so separable from all he had known, now be integral to all he has left. The print on the beach is both an image of trespass and a strong but necessary reminder that the castaway's life is unnatural because unsocial. Crusoe's fear initially renders him as wild as any being who might have made the print, that is, too native an inhabitant, one with no civilized history other than his island past: "I went on, but terrfy'd to the last Degree, looking behind me at every two or three Steps, mistaking every Bush and Tree, and fancying every Stump at a Distance to be a Man; nor is it possible to describe how many various Shapes affrighted Imagination represented Things to me in, how many wild Ideas were found every Moment in my Fancy, and what strange unaccountable Whimsies came into my Thoughts by the Way" (154).

Crusoe's first impulse is to measure the mark of the print against his foot. He even runs back to the beach to see if, indeed, the print belongs to him in the way the parrot's voice was a version of his own: "all this might be a meer Chimera of my own; and that this Foot might be the Print of my own Foot" (157). But reality dashes Crusoe's hope—the print is not his own stamp on a property he possesses unchallenged. Moreover, in an appropriate externalization of apprehension, the single print turns out to be too large. The other is not only different but bigger. For the fearful Crusoe, the mysterious impression on the beach assumes in size a power opposite to the self-diminishment he experiences on seeing it.

Crusoe finally gets the mark right, coming "out of all Apprehensions of its being the Devil: And I presently concluded then, that it must be some more dangerous creature, (viz.) That it must be some of the Savages of the main Land over-against me, who had wander'd out to Sea in their Canoes" (155). This sentence, with its wry secular wit, assumes that a very human cannibal poses greater danger to Crusoe than a doubtful devil. But Crusoe also recognizes the paradox of his lot.

> For I whose only Affliction was, that I seem'd banish'd from human Society, that I was alone, circumscrib'd by the boundless Ocean, cut off from Mankind, and condemn'd to what I call'd silent Life; that I was as one who Heaven thought not worthy to be number'd among the Living, or to appear among the rest of his creatures; that to have seen one of my own Species, would have seem'd to me a Raising me from Death to Life, and the greatest Blessing that Heaven it self, next to the supreme Blessing of Salvation, could bestow; *I say*, that I should now tremble at the very Apprehensions of seeing a Man, and was ready to sink into the Ground at but the Shadow or silent Appearance of a Man's having set his Foot in the Island. (156)

This passage not only reflects the conversional form of the novel, but its last phrase picks up the motif that Defoe has very craftily woven into the text from the beginning. The setting down of feet is crucial in a world that associates sovereignty with domain. The turning point of Crusoe's stay on the island, the point at which the slow process of opportunity begins to shape the true necessity for departure, is also the point at which the idea of his aloneness begins to take on different dimensions. The print is even more significant in its singleness: one print should suggest its complement, its other. To put the matter differently, Crusoe learns from the surface appearance of the footprint a deeper metaphoric lesson he ought never to have forgotten: no one ought to go it completely alone.

At first, the thought of penetration and potential cannibalism drives Crusoe nearly to despair. He lives a different and obsessed life on the island, spending most of his time hiding, disguising, burying, undoing. He even changes the essential nature of his exile, thinking no longer of the providential design of his history but of the barbaric isolation of the uncivilized: "I fancy'd my self now like one of the ancient Giants, which are said to live in Caves, and Holes, in the Rocks, where none could come at them" (179). Crusoe has been on the island for two decades, and he has managed to change his fable from the Jews in Sinai to the Homeric Cyclops.

After the sighting of the print, Crusoe is recidivistic. He wants to hide what he has made, to let nature take back its own forms. His massive tree planting campaign in two years produces an almost impenetrable forest in front of his habitation. Crusoe is aware of the obsessiveness of his fears and projects, but he cannot help himself. Sounding like Roosevelt of the Orinoco, he utters, "Thus Fear of Danger is ten thousand Times more terrifying than Danger it self" (159). His renaturalizing of the island is his paramount activity: "All this Labour I was the Expence of, purely from my Apprehensions on the Account of the Print of a Man's Foot which I had seen: for as yet I never saw any human Creature come near the Island, and I had now liv'd two Years under these Uneasinesses, which indeed made my Life much less comfortable than it was before; as may well be imagin'd by any who know what it is to live in the constant Snare of *the Fear of Man*" (163). Of course cannibals had probably been using the opposite side of his island the entire time he was on it without his knowledge. If Crusoe anticipates Roosevelt's "we have nothing to fear but fear itself," he might well have saved himself trouble by adapting the more banal, "what we don't know can't hurt us." Indeed, Crusoe's reasoning that the cannibals had been there, off and on, for years seems to calm him down; he returns to a semblance of his original island life, though he exercises prudence in firing of his gun and in ranging the island.

Crusoe goes from a subsistence to a deterrence economy. He worries constantly about campfire smoke; about the sound of hammering, or gunshot. He now truly lives what he had metaphorically called a silent life in reference to his aloneness. It takes him several years of defensiveness to get used to the notion that what seems to be his opposition might actually be the means by which he can alter his condition as a hopeless solitary and "Escape from this Place" (195). The fear of incursion makes his beloved settlement alien to him, a mere physical "Place."

Part of Defoe's project during the second half of Crusoe's stay on the island is to work through his castaway's fear. And he does so by reactivating a fictional construct that has already worked for him—he confronts Crusoe with yet another version of his own threatening and threatened self. More than twenty years into his stay on the island, Crusoe finds himself in a hollow burning wood for charcoal at which time he comes face to face with "two broad shining Eyes of some Creature, whether Devil or Man I knew not" (177). But this time he bucks up; he tells himself "that he that was afraid to see the Devil, was not fit to live twenty Years in an Island all alone; and that I durst to believe there was nothing in this Cave that was more frightful than my self" (177).

Though the creature lets out a "very loud Sigh, like that of a Man in some Pain," it turns out to be a dying he-goat, and Crusoe is not without the presence of mind to imagine his own future on the island by staring into the face of time: "I saw lying on the Ground a most monstrous frightful old He-goat, just making his Will, as we say, and gasping for Life, and dying indeed of meer old Age" (178). Here is an unviolated Crusoe on the one hand and an unrescued Crusoe on the other. There are trade-offs. To live like a goat is to die like one. In the parrot scene Crusoe hears his past; in the footprint scene he fears for the present; and in the old goat scene he projects his future. But there are other possibilities. Real men arrive on the island to substantiate voices in the air, prints in the sand, eyes in the dark.

Specifically, Friday arrives, a body to fill the print on the beach. Defoe sets up Friday's arrival with care, playing upon the symbols he has taught his readers to mark: feet and voices.

> I beckon'd him again to come to me, and gave him all the Signs of Encouragement that I could think of, and he came nearer and nearer, kneeling down every Ten or Twelve steps in token of acknowledgment for my saving his Life: I smil'd at him, and look'd pleasantly, and beckon'd to him to come still nearer; at length he came close to me, and then he kneel'd down again, kiss'd the

Ground, and laid his Head upon the Ground, and taking me by
the Foot, set my Foot upon his Head; this it seems was in token
of swearing to be my Slave for ever; I took him up, and made
much of him, and encourag'd him all I could. But there was more
work to do yet, for I perceived the Savage who I knock'd down,
was not kill'd, but stunn'd with the blow, and began to come to
himself; so I pointed to him, and showing him the Savage, that he
was not dead; upon this he spoke some Words to me, and though
I could not understand them, yet I thought they were pleasant to
hear, for they were the first sound of a Man's Voice, that I had
heard, *my own excepted*, for above Twenty Five Years. (203–4)

Crusoe cannot understand Friday but likes the sound of his
voice, the "first sound of a Man's Voice, that I had heard, *my own
excepted*, for above Twenty Five Years" (204). Whatever the status
of *"my own excepted"*—whether Crusoe talks to himself or dis-
qualifies the parrot—Friday's voice is now appropriated for island
life. So are his actions and the phrases used to describe them. When
the pair are soon threatened by the appearance of another force
from the cannibal main, Defoe repeats the motif of fear and footprints
that set Crusoe off in the first place: *"Friday* had not been long
gone, when he came running back, and flew over my outer Wall, or
Fence, like one that felt not the Ground, or the Steps he set his
Feet on" (230). The two islanders share clichés.

After Friday's arrival, and without precisely knowing why, Crusoe
assumes his deliverance is providentially opportune: "the great Hopes
I had of being effectually, and speedily deliver'd; for I had an invincible
Impression upon my Thoughts, that my Deliverance was at hand,
and that I should not be another Year in this Place" (229). Crusoe's
"Impression" that the times are ready for him seems as telling in its
way as the impression of the footprint years before. Crusoe loses his
fear of having his island trod upon when Defoe has him lose the
desire to protect domain that is no longer primed solely for his
holding of it. Even before Friday's arrival he had inklings of a new
order. That was why his disappointment was so severe when a second
ship, wrecked upon his island's shore, produced no survivors: "Pray

note, all this was the fruit of a disturb'd Mind, an impatient temper, made as it were desperate by the long Continuance of my Troubles, and the Disappointments I had met in the Wreck, I had been on board of; and where I had been so near the obtaining what I so earnestly long'd for, *viz.* Somebody to speak to, and to learn some Knowledge from of the Place where I was, and of the probable Means of my Deliverance" (198).

This is a complex passage. Prospects are something Crusoe must have; he is restless by nature. And company is something he now seems to need to ensure his prospects. So his silent life, so comforting to him in previous circumstances, becomes an obstacle. If potential rivals dominated his fears for nearly a decade, company as salvation now dominates his desires. He must be off this island and he needs help. The last phases of action in *Robinson Crusoe* provide that help. People drop in as if Crusoe is holding open house. It is no longer a question of a single print on the beach. Crusoe's island space has become a stomping grounds.

7

Island Writing

At the end of *The Autobiography of Alice B. Toklas* Gertrude Stein tells us that she writes for Alice "as simply as Defoe did the auto-biography of Robinson Crusoe." Defoe can write the self as other because, as James Joyce said of Shakespeare, the writer is all in all. Autobiographical fiction is always the autobiography of the powers of the imagining mind in which experiences, voices, and sensibilities are inextricably mixed. So when Charles Gildon exulted in the very year of *Crusoe*'s publication that he discovered Father Daniel in Son Robinson, that Crusoe was "the true Allegorick Image of thy tender Father D - - - - l" (Gildon, x), he stumbled upon a principle that allies writer and character in a complicitous exercise of self-projection, which, in some form or another, serves the novel for the next two and a half centuries, from Gustave Flaubert absorbing his most famous heroine, "Madame Bovary c'est moi," to Joyce "self-exiled in upon his own ego" in *Finnegans Wake*.[18] Gildon's hostile surmise about *Crusoe* is therefore worth considering. Much in the text lends him support.

From Defoe's point of view, adopting Crusoe as a second self makes fiction into a kind of personal history. The first piece of writing Robinson Crusoe produces, apart from a hasty double-entry account list of the miseries and opportunities of island life, is an entry in his journal that dates his arrival upon the island, supposing, of course, that the journal he writes predates the larger account produced by that same Crusoe in the book as a whole: "September 30, 1659" (70). Crusoe later tells his readers that his arrival date is also his birthday, leading biographers to suppose, with the other evidence being slight, that Defoe was born on 30 September as well, more likely in 1660 than in 1659. When Crusoe later recalculates his date of arrival, he says he may have been off a year in the figuring, producing a nagging suspicion that Defoe may have also gone astray somewhere on the exact year of his birth. Whatever the case, it is clear that from the beginning of the history of this remarkable volume Crusoe and Defoe are imaginatively and, in many ways, actually connected. There is a "strange Concurrence of Days, in the various Providences which befel me" (133), says Crusoe, who knows that he at least was born on 30 September and arrived on his island that day as well.

An inaugurating date links writer and character in an exercise of self-expression that generates a new form of literature—the novel—for an audience that was then, as it still is now, absorbed by it. But the September concurrence is just one kind of self-authoring. From his early family life, under the aegis of religious interdictions by the Stuart kings falling just short of outright persecution, up to the time he began writing *Crusoe, Moll Flanders, Colonel Jack*, and his other novels, Defoe lived what he called, in his condensed autobiographical confession, *An Appeal to Honour and Justice* (1715), a life of "Causeless curses, unusual Threatnings, and the most unjust and injurious Treatment in the World" (1). Defoe and Crusoe are allies in the course of life's trials and traumas. Defoe thinks of himself as a metaphorical survivor, and the metaphor is so striking for him that when he says, as he does on any number of occasions, that his life was a series of wrecks and recoveries he truly means it.

Robinson Crusoe was not the first time Defoe wrote himself into the story of presumed others. His long narrative allegory, a voyage to the moon in an engine called a *Consolidator* (1705), depicted a lunar philosopher pilloried and jailed for a tract much like Defoe's own *Shortest Way with the Dissenters* (1702). Defoe's early journalism and his midcareer experiments with the genre of advice literature—advice to families, to marriage candidates, to merchants, to governments—are also filled with vignettes of private and social life drawn from his own business and marital experience. When personal disasters, say that of the bankrupt wine merchant in *Essay upon Projects*, touch closely upon his own experiences, or, as he would put it in *Crusoe*, hit closely to home, they provide a special quality to Defoe's narrative fervor.

There is a recognizable charge in his writing when Defoe touches upon matters of immediate concern to his own life. Even the most common and ordinary events have a kind of hyperbolic import for him, and it is characteristic of his style to hear him speak in high dramatic contours about himself. Therefore when Crusoe points out during his Brazilian adventure, "and now increasing in Business and Wealth, my Head began to be full of Projects and Undertakings beyond my Reach; such as are indeed often the Ruine of the best Heads in Business" (37–38), readers are as much with the entrepreneur Defoe in 1690s boomtime London as with the merchant adventurer Crusoe in the remote world of colonial plantations.

Just to take one year in Defoe's early life, 1692, is to witness the pressures that would encourage him to weave allegories of disaster into his fiction. In his *Appeal to Honour and Justice,* Defoe claims this storm-tossed year was the result of a lost merchant ship during William's wars with France, but the truth is murkier. He was pursued on several fronts and dogged by lawsuits: one for not collecting contracted debts for a man named Braban; another for mismanaging his factoring responsibilities for another ship, the *Batchelor,* when it disgorged and tried to reload in Maryland; another for fraud in trying to corner the civet-cat perfume market in London; another for bilking a man out of his patented invention for recovering buried treasure; and another for trying to cash a bill of exchange drawn on a man killed in a duel.

Defoe was completely desperate; he even tried running an illegal shipment of block-tin to France, England's declared enemy at this time. In October of 1692 a writ of seizure was issued against his perfume-producing civet cats housed at Newington. Defoe tried to keep the business in the family by selling the civet-cats to his mother-in-law. Those pursuing him saw through that ruse and sued. Defoe was in arrears approximately £17,000, and some of his creditors refused legal settlement short of complete repayment. He had to use whatever resources he had and all his savvy to stay out of prison for debt, though there were occasions in October and November of 1692 when he was held over at the Fleet and King's Bench prisons before being released for court appearances. For the next few years he lived in his own land as a virtual outlaw, subject, as he wrote, to "Crowds of Sham-Actions, Arrests, Sleeping Debates in Trade" (*Defoe's Review*, 7 July 1705, 2:214).

For Defoe, the notion of vulnerability and potential ruin was part of his human condition, and he wrote about it incessantly, designing his major prose narratives, *Robinson Crusoe*, *Moll Flanders*, *Colonel Jack*, and *Roxana*, to reflect it. In his life he reserved for himself not the right so much as the necessity to take desperate measures to counter desperate situations, and his fictional characters do the same. Necessity colors personal behavior. The way an individual reacts to personal crisis is Defoe's subject in his fiction, never more graphically so than in *Crusoe*. Crusoe is a wreck. Only on his island and in isolation can he recover and reconstitute his person and his property. Defoe at several key times in his life wished as much for himself and says so in his prefaces to the subsequent *Crusoe* volumes. For instance, he wonders in the preface to *Serious Reflections* if any should suppose "the scene which is placed so far off, had its original so near Home" (*Works*, 3: xiii). It is difficult to know exactly what Defoe means here when he writes in Crusoe's voice and would seem to be doubling up on Crusoe's story as if it happened in two places at once, which is, I think, a possible reading of the narrative, a reading Defoe supports when he calls his narrative an "allusive allegorical history" (*Works, 3:* 107). Much of the confusion in these prefaces about whose story Defoe actually tells, Crusoe's or his own, is accounted for by the recurrence of disaster in Defoe's life and the vividness of his depictions of it in fiction.

Defoe's language on the matter of intermeshed lives in *Crusoe* deserves a look. There are a number of leading clues that Crusoe's lot is a version of Defoe's. In reference to the paradox that the island has delivered him, Crusoe says that "I cou'd give many Examples of this in the Course of my unaccountable Life" (181). What does unaccountable mean? That his life cannot be accounted or narrated? Or that it has not yet? Or that the decisions he makes and the inclinations that guide him are compulsive even if he ends up benefiting from them? Or that the accountable life is Crusoe's, and the unaccountable one, the one that is buried in the narrative, is Defoe's? To narrate that which is unaccountable is a strange reflex. But it is a reflex that makes the realistic novel one of the most engaging of genres. There are always double sets of events in realism—the sequence of actions that constitute the contingent and probable details of a life story and the potential allegorization of those actions into patterns or pressures that are universal in application, that are determined by forces of history or powers of motive shared by human beings in a human world. Defoe's writing of his own general story into Crusoe's specific one opens a vein in the history of the novel mined thoroughly by future novelists from Dickens in *Great Expectations* to Proust in *Remembrance of Things Past.*

If *Crusoe* is, at least in some measure, the life of Defoe, then his autobiography is, at least in some measure, the history of a narrator. Crusoe's adventure is a tale just brimming with the energy of the protagonist's desire to relay it in every way he can. He repeats his trials over and over again to himself, as if his telling makes him into his own book: "I run over the whole History of my Life in Miniature, or by Abridgment" (196). He finds a number of ways to write his actions and their meaning down, and he tells his story to whomever will listen: "In a Word, I gave them every Part of my own Story" (277). That he could do it in a word is doubtful. He never does. Telling a tale for Crusoe is as important as living its events. He senses the need to begin a detailed account of his island adventure all over again on any number of occasions. After narrating his first breather upon struggling to land on his island and stocking himself for his stay, he continues: "And now being to enter into a melancholy Relation of a Scene of silent Life, such perhaps as was never heard of in the World before, I shall take it from its Beginning, and continue it in its Order" (63). It is not surprising that a scene of silent life should be unheard of, but to be a "Relation" it must be heard or, at least, read. What Crusoe is describing here is the scene of narration, an Aristotelian one at that, with a beginning, a middle, and an end. The silent life is finally heard by Defoe's account in Crusoe's name.

In a very real way, *Robinson Crusoe* is a tale of telling. The things Crusoe does on the island are an emblem for the things the writer does with space and time in the realistic novel: account for them. To tell, as anyone who has ever waited in line for a teller at a bank knows, means to count as much as it means to narrate. And Defoe must be aware of the overlap, the merging of his "account" and his narration when he actually presents on the page of the book a ledger sheet written up by Crusoe to assess the situational and moral condition of his isolation. Crusoe organizes his story by tallying his lot and balancing his books. In case readers should be so obtuse as to miss it, he provides the account ledger as an artifact printed out on the page in double columns and introduced as an epitome of the larger action conveyed in the whole of the narrative: "I drew up the State of my Affairs in Writing" (65). The double-entry account serves a psychological need for Crusoe early on the island, but it is also Defoe's way of hinting that he knows his narrative is actually about the processes of telling or accounting stated "like Debtor and Creditor" (65). I cite only the first entries of a full page:

EVIL.	GOOD.
I am cast upon a horrible desolate Island, void of all hope of Recovery.	*But I am alive, and not drown'd as all my Company was.*
I am singl'd out and separated, as it were, from all the World to be miserable.	*But I am singl'd out too from all the Ship's Crew to be spar'd from death; and he that miraculously sav'd me from Death, can deliver me from this Condition.*
	(66)

The page here not only looks like a credit/debit sheet, an account in its most minimal and radical guise, but the telling reproduces the conversional motif of the narrative where one kind of experience turns into another. This is the way Crusoe thinks and Defoe writes. The attention paid to the look of details is the way writing verifies itself. Defoe's tallyings and tellings are part of his style, part of the circumstantial realism that sustains him. Crusoe, Friday, and the freed Spaniard kill cannibals, and the printing press partakes of the day's carnage.

The Account of the Rest is as follows;
3 Kill'd at our first Shot from the Tree.
2 Kill'd at the next Shot.
2 Kill'd by *Friday* in the Boat.
2 Kill'd by *Ditto*, of those at first wounded.
1 Kill'd by *Ditto*, in the Wood.
3 Kill'd by the *Spaniard*.
4 Kill'd, by being found dropp'd here and there of their Wounds, or kill'd by *Friday* in his Chase of them.

4 Escap'd in the boat, whereof one wounded if not dead.

—

21 In all.   (237)

Defoe has come a long way from the prose romance of earlier times when someone with the secretarial name of "Ditto" receives credit for sharpshooting. But this is of a piece with so much else in the story. Everything is accounted for, recounted, counted up—the days, weeks, years of island life, the careful accumulating and listing of supplies, the kernels of seed, the contents of packets of letters, the numbers of wolves in Spain. Who tells counts in Defoe's material world, and the telling is also what counts. Moreover, the effort to produce written documents that testify to Crusoe's story is part of the material process of narrating for Defoe. In arranging his life for the literary market, Crusoe has to arrange his papers. *Robinson Crusoe* is, in this sense, not only a primer on how to live on a remote island, but on how to write the experience up.

Certification by writing reflects one of the key strategies of the novel form in general as it struggles during the eighteenth century to distinguish itself from the more free-flowing heroic narratives of the previous century. Unlike famous romance or epic heroes who live in the communal memory, novelistic characters are private beings who come to life only by the written record that makes them public. To authorize that record, early novelists tend to surround their creations with supporting documents or to make the written life tantamount to the lived one. Samuel Richardson's Clarissa is the sum total of collated packets of letters that authenticate, register, and authorize her life and sentiments. More graphically, Laurence Sterne's Tristram Shandy cannot die, no matter how gravely ill, unless the written documentation of his life catches up to the number of years he has lived.

Defoe is the writer who began such documentary substantiation in earnest. To emphasize how important written documents are to

Crusoe's island experience, Defoe provides three real or implied written versions of the story: the editor's volume that readers read, Crusoe's manuscript that the editor reads, and excerpted journal entries interspersed with Crusoe's and the editor's version of the text. Writing on his island is an activity that enlists some of the same powers of organization, selection, accumulation, and application that Crusoe engages in to live on it. The journal is especially intriguing in this regard. It is only after Crusoe has ransacked the wrecked ship for all he could take out of her that he begins to keep his journal. This writing is given its own niche in the larger manuscript: "I shall here give you the Copy [tho' in it will be told all these Particulars over again]" (69).

Though Crusoe's raw material as a journalist is there for the reckoning, Crusoe as narrator reserves the right to break into the journal with commentary to allow information subsequent to the journal's writing to qualify matters or supersede them: "N. B. *This Wall being describ'd before, I purposely omit what was said in the Journal*" (76). This interweaving makes the journal entries actual artifacts of island life at the same time they are dispensed on the page by postisland narrators and editors. That is, the journal appears on the printed page of *Robinson Crusoe* as part of the accumulated paraphernalia that make up Crusoe's experience, and also as part of his later record for remembering it. The very look of the text thus partakes of the structure of the book, where sequential details give way, on occasion, to commentary. The journal also stands as a kind of synecdoche or part for the whole—it establishes the bona fides of the narrative that surrounds it.

By making the journal an entry of sorts into the larger narrative, Defoe can write time in two senses, the mimetic time of the experience and the reflective time that writing produces or encourages. The process reveals to the reader the kinds of transformations that take place between the recording of events in a story and the understanding of events that constitute the novelistic telling of that story. Mimetic journal time is documentary, dating the action; reflective narrative time is retrospective, patterning the action. It is almost as if the text of *Robinson Crusoe*, at least during the early island years, replicates Defoe's writing career as a daily journalist and a leisurely novelist.

When his ink begins to fail him, though he keeps a small reserve for later writings, Crusoe can conveniently break off the journal that he might well have published, had he written it completely, in lieu of his narrative. He begins to wind down after a year, including only "the most remarkable Events of my Life, without continuing a daily *Memorandum* of other things" (104). At first the record is sequential, soon it is remarkable, and, finally, it becomes a selective series of memoranda. Memoranda, of course, are strewn all over the island. In the Protestant tradition of autobiography to which *Crusoe* belongs, an individual's life is an open book, and the signatures of all things are there for the reading. After Crusoe spends years hacking out a canoe that he cannot transport to the water, he lets it remain in place (as if he had much choice): "I was oblig'd to let it lye where it was, as a *Memorandum* to teach me to be wiser next Time" (136). Crusoe will experience an even more effective signature or memorandum on the text of his island when he sights the famous footprint on the sand fifteen years into his stay. That imprint marks his life for a decade and sends so important a message that it turns the course of the entire narrative in its track. But the print stands as a hieroglyph and remains inexplicable, finally, because no one either knows or tells its full story. Crusoe's story, on the other hand, gets told and written over and over again, because its originator ends by writing up the island on which he was castaway.

8

Fathers and Sons

One of the more revealing qualities for Defoe about the way people behave is the limited understanding they have concerning the decisions that end up controlling them. Robinson Crusoe is fated to leave home for a life as a merchant adventurer. There is little anyone, including himself, can do about it. Of his "rambling Thoughts," Crusoe points out that there is "something fatal in that Propension of Nature" (3) that he cannot stifle or avoid. But in the logic of Defoe's vision of things, fate is also opportunity. Crusoe may later blame himself for ignoring "the Advice of my Father, the Opposition to which, was, *as I may call it,* my ORIGINAL SIN" (194), but that is only half the story. Crusoe had shown no inclination to obey anyone ever, and his nature is sinful only in terms of the strictures of condemnation he places upon it. For the writer of fiction, impulses, inner drives, restlessness are far more compelling than sins. The former are a function of character; the latter a reflex of belief.

The tension between what Crusoe's father called the settled condition and what Crusoe calls his "wandering inclination" makes for the fictional adventure in Defoe's novel. Crusoe's inner drive contravenes not simply the wishes of his father but any static design whatever in his life. He is a man on the move. The original version of his family name, Kreutznaer, means crusading traveler.[19] Almost as a psychological dependence, he is given "Sometime for a Ramble one way, sometimes another" (194). Crusoe's father may well advise his son to stay put in one place in a way that many merchant fathers might, and Defoe could understand the prudence of such sentiments. But Crusoe is not just a merchant. He is a merchant-adventurer. Defoe likes to double up in naming what his characters do, and the doubling provides the structure for their stories. In *Moll Flanders,* Moll is both mistress and wife, gentlewoman and thief, lover and sister. Double roles imply a kind of jeopardy, where one impulse in a character is at odds with another, prudence with adventure, insularity with wanderlust.

Crusoe spends much of the narrative bewailing his refusal to listen to his father's forceful request that he settle at home; yet all of his breast beatings are ironic in that had he the inclination to do what his father asked he would not have had the character to sustain the narrative he is in. Defoe reveals as much in subtle ways. To recall the family contretemps that begins Crusoe's narrative is to intuit something of the psychological register of the novel. Crusoe's father actually nullifies, or tries to, the story Defoe has to tell, which is not only about the fate that befalls Crusoe but about the nature of the impulses that drive him.

The same pattern of family separation and resistance manifests in an opposite, but still parallel, way in Defoe's *Journal of the Plague Year* when H. F. stays in London during the worst of the bubonic infection. He recognizes the folly of his action—the rest of his family are long gone to the country—but he stays because he is curiously compelled to see and experience for himself. He cannot change his nature to accommodate either another's will or even common sense. A person for Defoe has no distinction, really, until events are filtered through his or her consciousness, until impulses, desires, inclinations are fully played out. Defoe's fictional characters act on compulsion; that is their lot. The difficulties, risks, and traumas that accrue are the stuff of narrative. Crusoe, Moll Flanders, Roxana, and H. F. of the *Journal of the Plague Year* either make something of themselves in spite of their inclinations or, in a favorite Defoe word, are undone.

From the first, Crusoe responds one way to his father's advice and acts in another. He leaves home for a short sail to London without asking "God's Blessing," and after a brief storm he has all sorts of reservations about what providence has in store for him. Defoe offers up a bit of characteristic tight-lipped irony by having Crusoe report, "My Conscience, which was not yet come to the Pitch of Hardness to which it has been since, reproach'd me with the Contempt of Advice, and the Breach of my Duty to God and my Father" (8). But the pitch of hardness to which Crusoe refers is rarely a quality that he exhibits. What defines him is not a hard conscience but a changing, mercurial one. He feels deeply about things, but only on a moment's notice. He is given to radical shifts in emotion and a tendency to confuse what he is inevitably going to do with what he thinks he ought to do. In this first instance, a little sunshine on the sea deflects the reproach of Crusoe's conscience; he does not so much defy his father as dismiss the force of his concern.

Not only is Crusoe unwilling, virtually unable, to heed his father, but he ignores other advice—less biased and more ominous—that ought to have given him greater pause. After his first shipwreck in the Yarmouth Roads, young Crusoe hears from his companion's seaman father that he is bad news: "I would not set my Foot in the same Ship with thee again for a Thousand Pounds" (15). This old salt puts his mouth where his money is. Stay-at-home advice from Crusoe's father may be a family platitude; from an accomplished seaman it is a sobering premonition. But young Crusoe, though he runs scared, continues to run his own course. This leads some critics to deem Crusoe's sin as rashness rather than disobedience.[20] Late in his life, Defoe wrote a two-volume conduct book for merchants, *The Complete English Tradesman* (1725), in which he emphasized, as he did intermittently in his writings, the downside of rashness: "He that is above informing himself when he is in danger, is above pity when he miscarries: a young Tradesman who sets up, thus full of himself, and scorning the advice from those who have gone before him, like a horse that rushes into the battle, is only fearless of danger because he does not understand it" (v).

Whatever shape Crusoe's "sin" takes, the contempt with which he considers the original option to settle him in business, though never exactly articulated, is strongly felt. When Crusoe begins to make a go of it on his Brazilian plantation he comments, as if he has subverted his own impulses, that "I was coming into the very Middle Station, or upper Degree of low Life, which my Father advised me to before; and which if I resolved to go on with, I might as well ha' staid at Home" (35). Then he expresses what for him is real enough anguish, however much he fails to grasp the central impulse of his nature: "As I had once done thus in my breaking away from my Parents, so I could not be content now, but I must go and leave the happy View I had of being a rich and thriving Man in my new Plantation, only to pursue a rash and immoderate Desire of rising faster than the Nature of the Thing admitted" (38).

Crusoe's story dramatizes how difficult it is to make personal behavior conform to abstract principles of conduct, or, more significantly, how difficult it is to adjust personal psychology to rational action. Even though Crusoe pursues his "rich and thriving" life, ambition is not truly the mark of his character. In fact, ambition has as little to do with Crusoe as hardness of conscience. He is always slightly off in his self-condemnation. What is on his mind here is not the gain of plantation estates but a kind of settlement anxiety. The impulse that propels Crusoe to leave his plantation derives from the boredom that would depress him should he stay. To call such an impulse his original sin is at best a didactic vestige for Defoe, something like Hamlet thinking that the immense complexity of his psychological dilemma at Elsinore is attributable to sloth.

Defoe has his own suspicions about the advice Crusoe's father offers, and he reveals them by the subtleties of presentation. In fiction details are worth scrutiny because they always count for something. When Crusoe's father meets with his son near the beginning of the narrative to praise the virtues of the sedentary life, "He call'd me one Morning into his Chamber, where he was confined by the Gout, and expostulated very warmly with me upon this Subject" (4). The image is striking; an old man with gout, a sedentary disease, tells a young man with a wandering inclination what to do. A gout-ridden father sitting in front of Crusoe in many ways cancels the appeal of the advice. Gout is the luxury of caution. The "Life of Ease and Pleasure" that Crusoe's father represents is, after its own fashion, plagued. That notion contributes to the settlement anxiety Crusoe feels in England, in Brazil, and later even on his island toward the end of his stay. Crusoe's nature is not to sin in any real sense, but to feel strangely placed and anxiously located.

There is more in the first confrontation on the settlement issue between Crusoe and his father. The elder Crusoe asks his son "not to play the young Man" (5), but what sort of advice is that? Crusoe is a young man. Not to be one's self is a risky business in fiction. Though Crusoe listens to his father's advice, he only adapts it for a brief spell: "But alas! a few Days wore it all off" (6). His reaction marks a pattern: the intensity of an experience for Crusoe exists in proportion to the immediacy of the stimulus that produces it. Defoe's "alas!" is a key word here; it neither admits of real belief nor palliates real emotion. Alas is almost a sigh; it marks a kind of inevitability that, soon enough, is confirmed. After young Crusoe's embarrassing first trip to London and the foundering of his ship in Yarmouth Roads, he is ashamed to return to Hull: "As to going Home, Shame opposed the best Motions that offered to my Thoughts" (15). But when he ships out and takes passage on a Guinea voyage to the west African coast, it seems as if he has managed to finagle start-up funds with the tacit consent of family and relatives: "This 40 £. I had mustered together by the Assistance of some of my Relations whom I corresponded with, and who, I believe, got my Father, or at least my Mother, to contribute so much as that to my first

Adventure" (17). These starter funds, after the last the reader has from Crusoe's father is that he "can give no Consent to" (7) his son's rambling schemes, suggest that Robinson's original sin is partially absolved by some parental backsliding.

Defoe validates this very process in one of the first narratives he wrote after the *Crusoe* saga, *Memoirs of a Cavalier* (1720). In that protonovel he resists the notion that family members need stake out different positions about the prospects of children and then, come hell or high water, stick to them; rather, Defoe lets the members of a family negotiate for lines of power. Though the future Cavalier's mother and father oppose the wishes of their son to travel, they work out a compromise that, at least in its initial design, allows the son a year's trial run. Any reader of *Robinson Crusoe* too quick to credit the father's will that young Robinson stay at home might consider that Defoe always preferred rational negotiation to steadfast insistence. Individual character cannot define itself by the strict imposition of another's will. No model of action that demands absolute obedience to anyone is tenable unless that desire replicates one's own.

Defoe's hedging on the question of parental will touches on a theme of immense interest in the later seventeenth and early eighteenth centuries: the extent of familial and political authority. Too often family matters were confused, intentionally and otherwise, with political ones, or, more precisely, the model of action appropriate to families was confused with the model of action appropriate to the state. For Defoe, filial obedience is not a legal sanction but an obligation open to negotiation. To conceive of it in any other way is to approach an argument about the absolute power of the civil authority centered on the right of fathers in families. All his life Defoe opposed such an argument, and opposed it strenuously in his twelve-book political poem in verse, *Jure Divino* (1706). The question in *Crusoe,* as in almost all of Defoe's works, is not so much what happens when one resists authority as what happens when traditionally formed class values are juxtaposed against the drives, impulses, inclinations, and desires of particular individuals. It is in this very area that the novel, past and present, finds its most fascinating subject matter.

Whatever Crusoe says he feels about his own precipitous departure from home—and he never does quite sort out sin from impulse—his character may be better served in the long run by resisting his father's advice than by giving in to it complacently. There are times when the secure and complacent life he recommends is worse than the necessary errantry of a free soul. And it almost follows that the measure of Crusoe's hard-won settlement on his island is the degree to which his impulses force him to avoid too easy a settlement at home or in Brazil. Some of the best of recent work on *Crusoe* by young scholars, such as Richard Braverman and Christopher Flint, see the struggle of Crusoe as the struggle of the new order in English commercial or civic life, an order based not so much on family relations and custom as on proprietary contract and economic expansion. For Flint, the annulment of the family is a paramount experience in the whole of the *Crusoe* saga and made a necessity of island life. Island life, that is, becomes the symbol of what Crusoe seeks and needs all along: independence.[21]

The design in *Robinson Crusoe*, as James Joyce later puts it for all narratives involving the clash of fathers and sons, is based on a sense of physical separation that is also a psychological and material promise: "Where there is a reconciliation . . . there must have been first a sundering" (*Ulysses*, 159). Much of Defoe's fiction details the way individual human impulses separate characters from their surroundings and their families as a step toward personal reconstitution and refashioning. But Defoe does not stint on the risks involved: Moll Flanders's alienation from family results in incest; Roxana's in a possible infanticide; Crusoe's in a symbolical patricide. Crusoe kills the will if not the body of the father. When he later seeks the slave-trade venture rather than remain on his Brazilian plantation, the oedipal nature of the drama he enacts becomes clear: "But I that was born to be my own Destroyer, could no more resist the Offer than I could restrain my first rambling Designs, when my Father's good Counsel was lost upon me" (40). Destiny takes over from choice. Crusoe is his father's psychological opposite, and he is in a kind of temperamental rivalry with him.

There is another way to look at Crusoe's supposed disobedience that touches on the wider fictional matter of character formation. I mean this in both senses of writing up a character for fiction and of giving that character substance and integrity. To put it simply, Defoe would have had no narrative if Crusoe followed his father's advice; more important, his merchant hero would have had little character. James Sutherland makes a general remark on Defoe's temperament that bears on this issue: "If Defoe had not every kind of courage, he certainly had an unusual audacity. He continued all his life to take chances with those in authority, to run risks that a timid man would never even have contemplated" (*Defoe,* 87). The imp of resistance in Defoe is activated by the mere whiff of contravention. Inside Defoe's soul is some kind of demon of contrariness, and he often finds a way to let it loose in his fictional spaces.

Crusoe is hardly the one to give in on anything until he is the one who wills to do so. When on his island he considers the problem of getting material from the shipwreck to the beach without a ship's small boat he notes: "It was vain to sit still and wish for what was not to be had, and this Extremity rouz'd my Application" (49). "Sit still" is a charged phrase; it is precisely what Crusoe cannot do. In fact, the entire sentence could be rephrased to apply to the whole of the narrative: It was vain to sit still and wish for what was not to be. Although he repeatedly wrings his hands in mock despair at refusing to follow a course of which he was incapable in the first place, he also intermittently reveals his true nature often through observations seemingly detached from his original sin. Even Crusoe's innocent remark about failing to brew beer on the island reflects on his original refusal to stay at home: "I seldom gave any Thing over without accomplishing it, when I once had it in my Head enough to begin it" (168).

It makes more sense with Crusoe to take the long view, as had one of his famous Protestant precursors, John Milton in *Paradise Lost*. Original sin in that epic is designated *felix culpa*, or fortunate fall. Life is a learning process and error becomes the very basis for salvation, if, indeed, salvation is in the cards at all. Therefore, Crusoe's errantry is less the punishment that fits his crime (though many still read it so) than the opportunity to redeem and substantiate himself in his own eyes. Crusoe makes the point as clearly as it can be made: "The Evil which in it self we seek most to shun, and which when we are fallen into it, is the most dreadful to us, is oftentimes the very Means or Door of our Deliverance, by which alone we can be rais'd again from the Affliction we are fallen into" (181). He repeats the formula later on the island, toward the very end of his stay, when he says of men as God's creatures "that in the worst Circumstances they have always something to be thankful for, and sometimes are nearer their Deliverance than they imagine; nay, are even brought to their Deliverance by the Means by which they seem to be brought to their Destruction" (252).

If Crusoe acts as his own theologian on his island, he also acts as his own psychologist. He knows what stirs him: "secret Hints, or pressings of my Mind, to doing, or not doing any Thing that presented" (175). He worries less about defining sin than about slighting "such secret Intimations of Providence, let them come from what invisible Intelligence they will, that I shall not discuss, and perhaps cannot account for" (176). At the end of his island stay, he behaves in a manner consistent with his character from the beginning, and inconsistent with a notion of reflexive obedience. He feels urges and inclinations, including one to leave that "came upon me with such Force, and such an Impetuosity of Desire, that it was not to be resisted" (198). Crusoe keeps repeating those impulses on the island that his nature is heir to. The island has not so much absolved him as continued him.

9

Isle of Providence

Defoe is an intensely and persistently engaged writer on religious subjects, but that is not exactly the same as saying he is a religious writer, or, to put it more precisely, a spiritual writer. Defoe's fascination for and dedication to religious experience was lifelong, but inseparable from his interest in tangible, material human stories. His sensibility should not be alien territory especially for American readers in that the same materializing impulse of religious experience made the adventure of New England settlement into narratives of personal power and spiritual politics, narratives not altogether different from the one Defoe wished to provide his audience in *Robinson Crusoe*.

The fairest way to present Defoe's religious sensibilities in his fiction is to view his interests as rooted in the narrative forms they took. He is fascinated more by religious phenomena—ghosts, premonitions, second sights, visions—than by theological obscurities, doctrinal disputes, or the fine points of ritual practice. His interests in religion are almost always psychological rather than metaphysical. He prefers anecdote and illustration to preemptive admonition, and he has no stake in dogma for the mere exercise of it. Most important, he always factors into religious belief the human circumstances that sustain it, from Crusoe's inclination to develop religious precepts

91

during moments of terror and confusion to Moll Flanders's donning of penitence the way she might don a cloak.

However much Defoe saw religion as yet another subject for secular narration, he was still what his contemporaries labeled a dissenting or Puritan writer. Defoe's religious sensibility is commensurate with the radical strain in seventeenth-century religious life that struggled to come to grips with God's will seemingly disposed as secular circumstance. Every life is an ongoing text, a living text, an evolving text, producing a sequence of readable events and interpretable choices subject to constant religious revaluation. Even when he writes of afterworlds or the otherworlds, as he sometimes does, Defoe centers his imagination on motives and pressures he would recognize from the world in which he lives, the world of the here and now. Religion takes local shapes and local habitations; it is never divorced from the practical realities of life. And religious issues— obligation, confession, repentance, obedience, temptation, guilt—manifest as part of the real world of human choice, human motive, and human conduct.

In Defoe's novels, characters back away from abstracts such as duty and virtue when they come up full force against the more pressing exigencies of life, those Defoe calls necessity. Necessity has a kind of primacy in Defoe's general assessment of human motivation. The rigors of religious performance can be deferred in the name of necessity until the comforts of religious belief can be enjoyed in the glow of opportunity. Defoe's religious sensibility is essentially practical, a mix of hard analysis and all-purpose moral sentiments that assess the usefulness of religious belief at particular times, in particular circumstances, and for particular people.

What is implicit in Defoe's narratives is that religious promise must never disappear completely in the face of contingent personal trials or disappointments because that would be a presumptuous confusion of an uncertain present with a future that is providentially disposed. This is the position Crusoe reaches on his island. An individual could, of course, meet with a bad providential design in the future, but what would be the point of Defoe framing such a story as a novel? Defoe does not fully presume to know God's will. He much prefers to assume that providence sets out a life in exemplary ways and that individuals ready themselves for that which reflects the likely intent of providence. Novels are, by their nature, conditional.

Perhaps the best way to glean some understanding of Defoe's position is to concentrate for a moment on one word that appears and reappears in *Robinson Crusoe: providence*, from the Latin *providere*, "that which is seen before." It stands in typical dissenting or Puritan theology as that pattern of life which is bound to occur as part of a design for life determined by fate, the fate of an individual's nature or the fate determined by God's knowledge of that individual's nature, which amounts to something of the same thing. God has designs on men and women, and those who fare best do so because their conduct and their choices ultimately conform to what was in store or provided for them in the first place. Defoe defines providence in *Serious Reflections,* where he also engineers a theory of fiction to reveal its operations in regard to Crusoe. Providence is "the operation of the power, wisdom, justice, and goodness of God by which he influences, governs, and directs not only the means, but the events, of all things which concern us in this world" (*Works, 3:* 187).

Of course the problem with this definition is that it combines a manifestation of human action with an assumption about divine motive. Providence determines the design of life, but the participant or witness to the ongoing action of life can only plot that design from moment to moment. This is to say what happens happens. Defoe was well aware of the bemusing ironies here, as when Crusoe theorizes himself into a state of confusion about the sprouting of corn near his preserve.

> It is impossible to express the Astonishment and Confusion of my Thoughts on this Occasion; I had hitherto acted upon no religious Foundation at all, indeed I had very few Notions of Religion in my Head, or had entertain'd any Sense of any Thing that had befallen me, otherwise than as a Chance, or, as we lightly say, what

pleases God; without so much as enquiring into the End of Providence in these Things, or his Order in governing Events in the
World: But after I saw Barley grow there, in a Climate which I
know was not proper for Corn, and especially that I knew not how
it came there, it startl'd me strangely, and I began to suggest, that
God had miraculously caus'd this Grain to grow without any Help
of Seed sown, and that it was so directed purely for my Sustenance,
on that wild miserable Place. (78)

The next moment Crusoe dismisses all this because he remembers
casting aside some chicken feed, which turned out to be these very
corn stalks. So is the sprouting accident or providence? Or is accident
part of providence? The corn episode is Defoe's way of saying that
the assessments from the human perspective of providential design
can never really get beyond a kind of interpretable guess. Providence
is what something (everything) must mean until something else comes
along that seems to mean something else. This is not inconsistent
with the more liberal heritage of providential thought from the early
Puritan in England to their American descendants in New England.
And there is something potentially funny about such notions. Defoe's
great admirer in France, Jean-Jacques Rousseau, toys with cosmic
comedy when he wonders one day about the odds of his salvation:

One day, when brooding on this melancholy subject, I began throw-
ing stones at the tree trunks, and this with my usual skill, which
meant that I hardly hit one. While engaged in this noble exercise,
it occurred to me to draw a sort of omen from it, to allay my
anxiety. "I am going to throw this stone," I said to myself, "at the
tree facing me. If I hit it, it is a sign that I am saved; if I miss it
I am damned." As I said this I threw my stone with a trembling
hand and a terrible throbbing of the heart, but so accurately that
it hit the tree full in the middle; which really was not very difficult,
since I had taken care to choose a very large tree very near to me.
Since then I have never doubted my salvation. (*Confessions*, 231)

What is characteristic about this passage is also characteristic of
Defoe's fiction. Characters do not set out to act in accord with

providence, no matter what they think or say they do; rather, they read their actions as providential. This is a different thing; it opens territory for two kinds of narrative depiction: one, a secularized sequence of events or incidents that take place in a supposed life; and two, a sequence to which ex post facto meaning or significance is attached. All of this is consistent with what Defoe said he was doing in *Robinson Crusoe,* when, in *Serious Reflections,* he spoke of his allusive allegorical history. History is the depiction of lived events; allegory is the interpretable quality of those events as if they are patterned by God. It is Defoe's genius to set history and allegory in fictional balance, to allow for providential readings but not to contrive them beyond the range of the probable. Ian Watt calls this realism, and he is right to do so. The interpretable design—providentially disposed—does not, and cannot, from the point of view of Defoe's characters, overshadow the sense of lives lived as personal histories. The experiential power of Defoe's narratives is never obscured by their providential import.

For Defoe providence is not merely theological. The word also has significance as the substantial basis for the action in the story. After all, what does Crusoe do? He provides for himself under duress and over time. To provide is the secular verb that derives from the same etymological source as the theological noun providence. And in a material and psychological sense provision is what so much of the *Crusoe* fable is about. Crusoe has to build up a real store around him; he has to provide for his own security; he has to be materially sheltered, stocked, shorn up before the theological notion of providence carries any kind of force in his thinking. That is the way Defoe works as a writer and perhaps also thinks as a dissenter. The connection between foreseen events, the pattern set by God for life, and the provisions necessary for living is central to Defoe's vision. Individuals learn to provide for contingent and preordained fates.

The way Crusoe approaches island life reinforces the double notion of providence in the fable. Those innumerable pages and diary entries of recording material saved from the wreck, food stored in secreted places, reserves of grain, trees planted, enclosures staked out suggest that Crusoe learns of what is providentially set for him primarily by learning to provide for himself. That is the theology of the book displayed, for Defoe's purposes, in the fictional subject of solitary island life. When in *The Farther Adventures of Robinson Crusoe* things go bad on the island, then populated by English and Spanish settlers, it is as if the island has a bad fate, its provisionary plans are faulty.

At first, Crusoe's sense of his earlier time on the island conveys a similar notion of bad providence. His initial serious leisure thoughts are shaky: "Why Providence should thus compleately ruine its Creatures, and render them so absolutely miserable, so without Help abandon'd, so entirely despress'd, that it could hardly be rational to be thankful for such a Life" (62). But Crusoe quickly realizes he is better off than others on the boat: "Why were you singled out?" (63). Defoe's radical Protestantism is beginning to seep through here. If life is providentially designed, its contours and its details are there to be queried and interpreted. For every why there is a wherefore, for every turn there is another turn, for every contingency there is a provision.

Crusoe develops his religious sensibility from the ground up. He blames his choice of merchant adventuring for his early attitude. The hazards of a life at sea inures the sailor by "a harden'd despising of Dangers" (131). This is precisely the kind of maritime machismo that also made it difficult in the late seventeenth century to convince underwriters to provide merchant insurance. There was a sense that the entire maritime enterprise was somehow a challenge to providence. Crusoe's father thinks along these lines as well. He may never say so exactly, but such a notion hovers behind his objection to his son's vocation.

Whatever religious or providential principles Crusoe cultivates on his island come through his experience as castaway, though Defoe is careful to adhere to the principles of fictional realism in this regard. Religion for Crusoe is a barely mediated word for crisis. He does the best he can as his own spiritual counselor, but Crusoe is of the immediate response school to theology, as when, after the shock of an earthquake, he utters *"Lord ha' Mercy upon me"* (80). This is more reflex than prayer. Crusoe's religion also has its comic propensities throughout the narrative. After imbibing a considerable quantity of an intoxicating tobacco and rum solution to aid his recovery from a devastating ague, Crusoe gets solidly buzzed and randomly opens the pages of a Bible he salvaged from the shipwreck. In his paranoid high any passage would have probably meant something to him. He hits on Psalm 50:15: *"Call on me in the Day of Trouble, and I will deliver, and thou shalt glorify me"* (94). This seems appropriate until he manufactures his own doubts by reading a little further and comparing himself to the murmuring Jews in Sinai who wonder in Psalm 78, *"Can God spread a Table in the Wilderness?"* or, as Crusoe puts it, "can God himself deliver me from this Place?" (94). Crusoe has obviously thought about obtaining his rescue even before religion enters in through the back door opened by demon rum. Maybe that is the point. All delivery is a kind of self-delivery, which may be what is meant by the notion that an individual is delivered by God.

In the middle stages of his island life, Crusoe begins to reinterpret the notion of deliverance to mean delivered to his island for salvation rather than delivered to it as a simple castaway. As he settles in, it begins to look more as if he was meant to settle in. The island is a personal and interpretable text primed for his conversion. His religious experience can be fairly well predicted from the run of Protestant ethics and common sense to which any Englishman of the time would have been exposed. Crusoe need do no more than piece together scraps of biblical text and his own personal signs of special providential delivery. "How wonderfully we are deliver'd," Crusoe thinks, "when we know nothing of it" (175). This is a recipe for total conviction about everything, the ideal state of the contemplative believer.

Crusoe's island religion counts on a series of tightly structured little apothegms that point a moral as they adorn his tale. These miniaturize the kind of conversion or turn that marks the larger fable. Any kind of revelatory experience is reducible or expandable in the general course of living a life designed by providence. I cite several of Crusoe's observations without reference to their particular contexts because, stylistically, they serve for all seasons: "there was scarce any Condition in the World so miserable, but there was something *Negative* or something *Positive* to be thankful for in it" (67); "All our Discontents about what we want, appear'd to me, to spring from the Want of Thankfulness for what we have" (130); "as my Life was a Life of Sorrow, one way, so it was a Life of Mercy, another" (132); "Thus we never see the true State of our Condition, till it is illustrated to us by its Contraries" (139); "How strange a Chequer Work of Providence is the Life of Man!" (156); and "O what ridiculous Resolution Men take, when possess'd with Fear! It deprives them of the Use of those Means which Reason offers for their Relief" (159).

Knottier religious matters than these are way beyond his ken, and Crusoe himself knows it. He protests to Friday that he is far from a doctor of divinity. But at the end of his adventures Crusoe can do better than perform as casuist; he can play God. When the English mutineers land in the last year of Crusoe's stay he recasts memories of first landing on his island of despair. He says the men are in like condition to himself, though they do not know and cannot imagine how "near it was to them, and how effectually and really they were in a Condition of Safety, at the same Time that they thought themselves lost, and their Case so desperate" (252). To follow out this reasoning puts Crusoe in relation to those just landed as providence was in relation to him. Or, at least, it puts Crusoe in the chain of deliverance higher than the natural order of things would allow. This possibility seems a magical reality when the true English captain first reacts to Crusoe and wonders whether he is talking to *"God, or Man! . . . Man, or an Angel!"* (254), though it's doubtful in the iconography of seventeenth-century life that either God or angels are depicted fully clad in goatskins with huge mustaches, long enough, by Crusoe's own reckoning, to hang a hat on. Nonetheless, and with Defoe's tongue slightly in his religious cheek, it is a pleasant thought for Crusoe to see himself as another's providence, to be able to do in a few hours for someone else what took twenty-eight years for him.

10

Economic Fables

Few critics today still read *Robinson Crusoe* as a simple fable of what Ian Watt calls *homo economicus,* or economic man.[22] Crusoe's dilemma on the island resists systematic economic analysis because everything is colored by his isolation. As a writer who thought about economic issues all his life, Defoe was well aware that economic systems do not consist of one man on an island. They consist of delicately calibrated relations among manufactures, labor sources, wages, prices, supply, demand, monetary circulation, trade agreements, debt structure, and exchange rates. None of these has a place on the island. Even Karl Marx refused to make an overreaching economic parable of Crusoe's island adventure, distinguishing carefully between a man alone and the more fully communal resources of normal social production: "All Robinson's products were exclusively the result of his own personal labour and they were therefore directly objects of utility for him personally. The total product of our imaginative association is a social product."[23]

In general, Defoe believed in a broad, national economic vision. Insular or local practices were anathema to him, often making economic practices redundant, contradictory, unaccountable, and baroque. He is humane and eclectic in his economics, valuing the work and well-being of human beings before the abstract twists and pulls of the marketplace. In his early *Consolidator* (1705), an allegory of British life projected onto a lunar voyage, he imagined an economic utopia in which sensible merchant interests, predominantly dissenters in religion, controlled national resources, protected a thriving market economy, established responsible regulatory agencies, and monitored the general well-being of the country. In an even earlier work, his very first full-length book, *An Essay upon Projects* (1697), he presented an economic program for thoroughgoing national reform in labor distribution, social welfare, public education, finance, trade, civil law, taxation, and maritime insurance.

All this is to say that *Robinson Crusoe* is not set up primarily to explore Defoe's national economic theories. But elements of his larger view express themselves in Crusoe's smaller circumstances. Economic and material negotiations for Defoe are part of what can be called the human contract; that is, they must be conducted on the basis of human trust and ethical obligation. People take care of Crusoe, from the Portuguese captain on the high seas to merchant owners of the ship he saves from mutiny in his island harbor to the authorities in Brazil overseeing his plantation for two decades.

Even earlier, when his ship foundered at anchor in Yarmouth Roads, a young Crusoe survived on goodwill. What is at issue in this instance is a communal rally from disaster, which is always Defoe's ideal for the social scene. Though Crusoe faints before the ship founders, he is among those rescued when a small boat takes the crew to shore. There were a "great many people running along the shore" (13) to assist. Crusoe is helped by locals, housed, clothed, and funded to ship back out from London or to Hull. The kindness of strangers in Defoe's moral and commercial universe is often paramount in the adventures he depicts.

Defoe provides another hint of his moral economy before the island experience when he has Crusoe describe the way the natives on the African coast react to his shooting a leopard. They understand that the beast now belongs to him, but when he lets them eat it they skin it for him and also give him their provisions, partly in exchange and partly out of friendship and gratitude. Perhaps because of Defoe's own dealings in the world of European trade and finance— and his sense of betrayal in these dealings by sneaks and snakes who took him in—moral worth, ethical reliability, friendly considerations, and decency are part of Defoe's economic ethics. His point that scoundrels spoil any system, from communal to national ones, is a theme that he comes back to again and again in his journalism and fiction, and he hints at it at the end of Crusoe's island stay when contracts can exist only among men of good faith. The rotten apples have to be temporarily taken out of the human barrel before Crusoe can cut a deal to remove himself from the island and settle his affairs. But the respite is brief. Because Crusoe does leave and the rotten apples, the remnant of English mutineers, stay on the island, the colony later collapses in a social economy guided by bad faith.

The economics of just desserts and long-standing obligation are even more apparent when Crusoe gets to Brazil and, later, when he hears of the disposition of his Brazilian plantations after his island rescue. Defoe's heroes and heroines usually end up capitalizing on the decent conduct of those who handle their affairs. They get what is coming to them—more, perhaps, than Defoe, who, as an entre- preneur in boomtime England got what others may have thought was coming to him, outlaw status as a bankrupt, surely not the security of a fortune or an estate. So if there is a parable of economic life in the narrative, its locus is Brazil. When Crusoe, having escaped from Moorish captivity, is picked up by the Portuguese ship off Cape Verde islands heading toward South America the captain takes exact inventory of things, "even so much as my three Earthen Jarrs" (33). The way Crusoe sets up the principles of *meum* and *teum*, rights and legal transfers, ownership and obligation is key to his vision of a moral economy that dominates the narrative. The moral notion behind things is what should hold firm in life, a system based on reason, on rights, and, most important, on generosity and obligation. Defoe's economics, like his politics, begins with the beating hearts of men and women. There is no economic dealing without moral law, without communal law. This is why Crusoe's holdings in Brazil do not evaporate with the passage of time.

Crusoe is able to parlay his resources well, and the whole of the Brazilian experience, before and after the castaway plot, is an instance of the kind of protective productivity Defoe emphasizes in his many economic schemes and projects over the years. First, Crusoe exchanges some of his money into tools and goods for use on his plantation. Everything falls into place. The captain's widow in England gives a gift to the Portuguese captain; he in turn purchases a servant for Crusoe; Crusoe extends a gift of tobacco to the captain. Crusoe then sells some of the English goods at four times their value. His capital is then converted to stock; the stock is sold beyond the value of the original capital. New capital is invested in land for production. His land can eventually produce more, and Crusoe "was now infinitely beyond my poor Neighbour, I mean in the Advancement of my Plantation" (37).

This all holds firm, after a fashion, for the decades Crusoe spends as a castaway on his island. His Brazilian estates are carefully tended and, finally, parceled out after twenty-eight years on the basis of a humane and intricate profit-sharing plan that benefits the colony, its inhabitants, the imperial economy, and the former proprietor, the rescued Crusoe. Moreover, the colonial government and even the Catholic church are the trustees for this English Protestant adventurer. This is as utopian as English writers get, and Defoe paid a price for the generosity he extended to the Iberian nature by some savage contemporary attacks at home on the quality of his patriotism.

When the scene of *Crusoe* shifts to the remote and isolated desert isle in the Orinoco basin, little like the Brazilian chain of events is possible, though the only language Crusoe has for his own productivity and progress as castaway might make it seem so. Crusoe's activities on his insular and sovereign domain are still in a general way centered on a kind of moral economics where labor, production, and utility are good for the soul. The sententiae of which Crusoe is so fond have particular significance to his condition: "That all the good Things of this World, are no farther good to us, than they are for our Use" (129). In this phase of production, Defoe finds things for Crusoe to do that make him a practitioner of primitive crafts more than an object of advanced economic theory. Defoe's biographers all claim that he admired the artisans and craftsmen of London, and in his own travel writing Defoe always took time to acknowledge the handiwork of regional England and Scotland. One of his earliest pieces was on the value of mechanical work and handicrafts for the well-being of the individual and the state, *A Discourse of the Necessity of Encouraging Mechanick Industry: Wherein it is plainly proved, That Luxury and the want of Artisans Labour, became the Ruine of the four grand Monarchies of the World* (1689). But it would be a bit foolish to apply such an admonition to Crusoe—his island kingdom is not at risk in this regard.

It would do better to chart Crusoe's island economy on its own territory. The story is less about production or even artisanship than it is about the relation of control to insecurity, expansion to hoarding, power to fear. Economic laws matter less than accumulation. Crusoe ends up producing more than he needs for subsistence because he wants to lay in against the future; he wants to live secure. Experience has taught him that he ought to cover his bets, and he spends a good deal of his time on the island developing backup stores and contingency plans. Defoe makes all this a natural concern on Crusoe's island.

It does not take long to see the protectionist ethic manifest in *Robinson Crusoe*. Having taken chances and suffered for them, Crusoe begins to take chances in a different way as his life and narrative progress. He learns not to take a step without a counterstep, not to entertain a thought without adding up the contingent risks and benefits. His mind is much like the double-entry bookkeeping chart he produces after his arrival on the island. For every deficit there is a benefit. The trick in life is to set the balance in one's favor. Most of Defoe's economics in *Crusoe* boil down to this notion. And most of Crusoe's actions reflect it. In his own life and in his many writings, Defoe made the notion of balance a position of advocacy. He knew that risk is an essential part of the life of the merchant adventurer, but sensible protection from disaster is necessary to stimulate a sensible element of risk. Defoe recommended everything from maritime insurance to social security, from trade and bankruptcy boards to workman's disability. He had good reason for his sentiments and his schemes in that his own life contained a surfeit of risk and a minimum of protection.

Economics for Defoe, as for Crusoe, is more a psychology than a system. For example, Crusoe himself says that his acquisitive impulse is obsessive. He takes everything he can from the shipwreck and would have secured every last piece of wood had the tides permitted. Much that he stores either provides little use to him or is, in subsequent years, ruined. But at the time he takes everything he can for two reasons: 1) he will never know about future use, and 2) the action of taking fills the seemingly limitless time he has at his disposal.

The reader gains a kind of cumulative thrill watching Crusoe at work. He adjusts from a monetary to a use economy by seizing the carpenter's chest, "much more valuable than a Ship Loading of Gold would have been at that time" (50). He takes what he later refers to as a "general Magazine" (69) from the ship: nails, a kind of screw-lift for raising heavy objects, a grindstone, crow bars, bullets, powder, loose clothes, a hammock, rigging and sail, rope, canvas, rum, sugar, flour, a hogshead of bread, cables, iron, masts (some of which he lost when his raft tilted), razors, scissors, knives, forks, pen, paper, compasses, dials, perspectives, charts, navigation books, three bibles, catholic prayer books, a dog, two cats, silver coin, and gold pieces of eight. "O Drug!" (57), he says at the sight of the money, but takes it anyway, as he does again years later when a second wreck presents itself off shore with three bags of pieces of eight, bars of gold, and six doubloons of gold among its store.

Much too much has been made of these money scrounging scenes, and they deserve comment in terms of Crusoe's specific situation. To read Crusoe's remarks on money as making a dramatic distinction between use economics and capitalist economics is possible but shortsighted. Crusoe understands that the money is of no immediate value, but he takes it for reasons that are obvious. He might need it in the future. Indeed, it comes in handy at the end of the adventure when his finances once again take on the contours of social legitimacy and economic leverage. He takes out all his money, tarnished by time, and shines it up, emphasizing not only the abstract points he had been making about money and use throughout, but a new application of his own labor, rubbing the coins all shiny new for good cause. Moreover, having kept his money, even whimsically all those years, may be a moral gesture that buttresses what Crusoe saw as a social (almost religious) obligation to counter the despair of isolation. To have chucked the money early would have been to assume the permanence of his condition, and he had real reasons to avoid that pitfall.

An interesting addendum to the moral economics of *Robinson Crusoe*, of course, is the introduction of the seemingly tangential issue of the slave trade. Slavery hovers like something of a curse over the narrative, though Defoe is of two minds about it. He is not oblivious to the necessity of slave labor for any plans the British may have to colonize Spanish territories, but his humanitarian impulses on the issue of slavery are akin to being against the treatment of the cocks in cock fighting but not against the activity itself. Defoe's attitude is regulatory not abolitionist. In *Colonel Jack* he devotes a good part of his narrative to reform of the slave and indentured servant system in America. He did not go so far as to condemn the practice because his sense of labor requirements was such that he feared economic stagnation in the New World without the slave system, but he did sense the inhumanity of it, and he contrived ways to write about that inhumanity. In *Robinson Crusoe* he says nothing. He merely has Crusoe, a classic actor in his own tragedies, cast ashore alone after a slave trade disaster. The scene itself speaks silently.

Crusoe is given to actions that might in a way counter the moral economy of the story. Not only is he on a slave-trade venture when he is castaway, but the earlier selling of the boy Xury touches an ironic key. Here is Xury, a lad whom Crusoe claimed had so much affection for him that he "made me love him ever after" (25), sold for less than the price of Crusoe's boat, though he would have liked him back when he needs help in Brazil—presumably as a slave, not under wages: "I had done wrong in parting with my Boy *Xury*" (35). Wrong here is an economic wrong not a moral one, something J. M. Coetzee realizes in his recent counterversion, *Foe*, when he has Crusoe (spelled Cruso) point out, " 'If Providence were to watch over all of us,' said Cruso, 'who would be left to pick the cotton and cut the sugar-cane? For the business of the world to prosper, Providence must sometimes wake and sometimes sleep, as lower creatures do.' "[24] In this regard it is no accident that in Defoe's original when Crusoe names Friday he also teaches him to call him Master "and let him know, that was to be my Name" (206).

Granted, neither Crusoe nor Defoe have excessive qualms about slavery, but the larger action in the narrative is set up in such a way that Crusoe appears to undergo some kind of penance for the moral vacuum of past actions. After all, slave trading and cannibal killing frame his island stay. Repatriation for Crusoe comes only after he deals with his own murderous impulses in light of cannibal rights, which are, by implication, natural rights for the natives of South America just as there ought to be natural rights for the native African. It is almost as if Crusoe has to get back to society by reworking the idea of rights and human obligations. This is not an unproductive way to read at least part of the action, though Defoe does not moralize excessively about any of these matters and would prefer, for reasons that affect international colonization, to avoid the issue of slavery altogether.

11

Style

Defoe's style sustains what has come to be a defining feature of the novel that differentiates it in large measure from the romantic and epic narrative forms that both precede and, in the early eighteenth century, compete with it. In *Rise of the Novel,* Ian Watt identifies that feature as circumstantial realism. What he means is that the prose of the early novel takes the time to reproduce highly probable actions in highly recognizable contexts. The symbolic import of these actions may be read into the narrative, but their probability is the writer's primary stylistic goal.

Even in instances where the action in *Crusoe* seems imbued with an allusive or symbolic style, the realistic impulse in Defoe's prose wins out. For example, when he is first hauling material off the shipwreck on a makeshift raft, Crusoe is aghast as the lowering tide runs his load aground, and it begins to shift on the raft. He stands for a half hour with his back against cargo. This is telling detail. Defoe could be letting his reader know, in a general sense, that Crusoe's back is indeed against it, but the physical image of the scene is as direct as any metaphoric significance. In fact, the desperation of a man trying to save the fruits of many hours work is what comes through most clearly: "I did my utmost by setting my Back against the Chests, to keep them in their Places, but could not thrust off the Raft with all my Strength, neither durst I stir from the Posture I was in, but holding up the Chests with all my Might, stood in that Manner near half an Hour, in which time the rising of the Water brought me a little more upon a Level, and a little after, the Water still rising, my Raft floated again" (51).

When he finally lands safely in the river inlet, Crusoe uses his oars as a landed anchor to hold position until the tide rises further and the raft can be moored with two other broken oars in the ground. I have already mentioned the possibility that this scene alludes to a more famous one in the Homeric *Odyssey*, the oar planting in the epic that marks the end of Odysseus' need to wander, but the way Defoe presents the action there is no strict need to recall the *Odyssey*. The scene is complete in and of itself, and compelling as descriptive realism: "All that I could do, was to wait 'till the Tide was at highest, keeping the Raft with my Oar like an Anchor to hold the Side of it fast to the Shore, near a flat Piece of Ground, which I expected the Water would flow over; and so it did: As soon as I found Water enough, for my Raft drew about a Foot of Water, I thrust her on upon that flat Piece of Ground, and there fasten'd or mor'd her by sticking my two broken Oars into the Ground" (52).

A similar instance is Crusoe's shooting of a lion in Africa. In epic or romance, the scene would be highly formulaic. But Defoe is fascinated by a sequence that is, first and foremost, probable. Crusoe angles for a shot with his biggest gun, "almost Musquet-bore" (27). Because of the way the lion is crouched the odds are against a clean shot at a vulnerable spot. Crusoe can hit the beast only with a blast in the leg. As the roaring lion reacts to the shot, he stands stunned, then buckles on his shattered leg. He finally presents in a way that grants Crusoe an open shot at his head. Crusoe takes his second piece, with a smaller bore, and drops the lion with a shot to the head. The young man, Xury, then finishes the beast off with a muzzle shot right behind the ear from close range. Defoe's effective final remark about Xury's practiced hunting reflex—it "dispatch'd him quite" (28)—does the lion in. Defoe allows himself the luxury of yet more detail. The lion's foot is hacked off by Xury as an emblem of the conquest; the beast is skinned because the skin might serve, as it later does, for a blanket. This brief but circumstantial passage about shooting and skinning a lion is a model for Defoe's fictional realism.

Defoe has not only a good sense of narrative detail, but a superb narrative ear. He is an extraordinary mimic—even getting thrown in jail for one of his more outrageous impersonations in print, *The Shortest Way with the Dissenters* (1702). One of the more pronounced elements of his style is the manner in which he picks up the natural speech rhythms of his subjects. Certain exchanges in *Moll Flanders* or in *Robinson Crusoe* seem as fresh as if they were uttered and recorded on the spot. Even dialogue that does little to advance the action lends something special to Defoe's narratives, something genuine. Early in *Crusoe*, young Robinson is upset with the brief storm off Hull, and even more so when his friend calls it *"a Cap full of Wind"*: *"A Cap full d'you call it?* said I, *'twas a terrible Storm"* (9). This has the authentic stamp of a neophyte mariner and conveys with an incredulous "d'you call it?" the disappointment that befalls a young salt upon the realization that the pressure of his own emotions does not fully register on another's barometer.

Much later in his adventure, indeed near the end of his island stay, an older Crusoe overhears the first words of native English he has heard in over a quarter of a century spoken by native English seamen. The cadences and the phrasings are natural and exact, and the scene comes alive because of it. One sailor on Crusoe's beach advises another about hauling in the longboat: *"Why let her alone, Jack, can't ye, she will float next Tide"* (253). It is hard to mark the effect here exactly, but it has a good deal to do with the dead on, *"can't ye."* This is the touch of a writer who listens to people talk. Defoe's years as a merchant, manufacturer, journalist, and spy made him sensitive to class and occupational idioms, and he records them with great success in his fiction.

Defoe achieves what Milton had called an answerable style, a style that suits the circumstances of his characters and the temporal settings of his narratives. That style can be amusing. In the following instance Crusoe gropes for an analogy to explain his fainting on the beach after his shipwreck: "I do not wonder now at that Custom, *viz.* that when a Malefactor who has the Halter about his Neck, is tyed up, and just going to be turn'd off, and has a Reprieve brought to him: I say, I do not wonder that they bring a Surgeon with it, to let him Blood that very Moment they tell him of it" (46). The reprieve is as charged as the sentence; the relief as shocking as the condemnation. But what makes the passage work, amidst the obligatory halters, surgeons, and bloodletting, is the wonderful "turn'd off," a bit of contemporary slang apparently as current in the criminal underworld then as it is now.

There are many other elements of Defoe's style worthy of comment, and Crusoe's early adventure along the African coast is a good place to continue noting them. While sailing near the shore, Crusoe and his young companion, Xury, hear the roars of a wild beast: "we could not see him, but we might hear him by his blowing to be a monstrous, huge and furious Beast" (25). The impression of a sound is enough to create an image. The beast is in Crusoe's mind. Furthermore, the sounds themselves are not readily conveyed in descriptive prose: "But it is impossible to describe the horrible Noises, and hideous Cryes and Howlings, that were raised as well upon the Edge of the Shoar" (25). Yet the noises, cries, and howlings have somehow been impressed upon Defoe's reader in the same way as the creature that made them. When Defoe defends fiction as a valid enterprise he does so on the basis that, as a writer, he can produce impressions that strike the imagination as real.

It is characteristic of Defoe's locutions that the very impossibility of describing something suffices for its realistic description. Stylistically, Defoe denies the impression he exaggeratedly creates. But he cannot be accused of imprecision so much as hyperbole. Defoe's style creates a kind of aura around experience, and he insists impressions can still be vivid even if words do not exactly evoke them. Another instance occurs soon after when Crusoe shoots a leopard in front of the African natives and records that it was "impossible to express the Astonishment of these poor Creatures at the Noise and the Fire of my Gun" (30). But the word *astonishment,* which means turns to stone, itself does part of the deed Defoe claims impossible. Or later, just before he is tossed onto his island, Crusoe recalls that "Nothing can describe the Confusion of Thought which I felt when I sunk into the Water" (44). Here the stark, archetypal power of the phrase "sunk into the Water" evokes the almost universally sensed confusion of the drowning body. Later yet, Crusoe combines the gist of former impossibilities when he expresses wonder at the corn stalks mysteriously appearing near his habitat: "It is impossible to express the Astonishment and Confusion of my Thoughts on this Occasion" (75). Of course, by now Defoe's readers know just what astonishment and confusion look like and feel like.

It is worth pursuing the first coastal adventure in Africa to elucidate other aspects of Defoe's style. When Crusoe fires a shot from his boat at the beast he could not see and could not describe he fears the sound will rouse the natives: "This Convinc'd me that there was no going on Shoar for us in the Night upon that Coast, and how to venture on Shoar in the Day was another Question too; for to have fallen into the Hands of any of the Savages, had been as bad as to have fallen into the Hands of Lyons and Tygers; at least we were equally apprehensive of the Danger of it" (25).

There is an incremental quality to Defoe's writing. He keeps coming forward: one questioning clause leads to speculative yearnings or doubts in another; one fear or apprehension produces others. Night fears lead to day fears. Fear of animals leads to fear of the natives. The mere formulation of ideas produces other ideas, and, when Crusoe gets around to recording the process in prose, the progress of his sentences resembles a mind receiving and arranging impressions. Passages such as the one quoted last mark Defoe's fiction.

His is not heavily descriptive prose, but it is heavily evocative prose, prose that registers reception and impression.

Another stylistic ingredient of realism, according to Ian Watt, is harder to mark: irony. Irony itself may be difficult to define, but its presence in most realistic fictions is incontestable. In a minimal sense, irony is the power of fictional language to reflect two sides of an action at the same time, to reveal alternative and even contradictory nuances of experience, to play out scenes in two time zones, the immediate and the reflective. Learning to read irony—to see the opposing sides of an action and to gauge the modulations of language describing it—is to learn how characters work and think in fiction.

An engaging instance in Defoe's fiction of a strong ironic hand occurs near the beginning of *Moll Flanders* when Moll learns to distinguish between passion and payment. The sequence is a brilliantly paced and ironically charged bit of social reflex that readies the heroine for a more savvy and shrewd material arena of love. Moll is deeply in love with the eldest brother of a provincial household who, every time he gains her favors, leaves a few gold coins on the illicit couch. Slowly, tantalizingly, inexorably, Moll's language of romantic love turns financially savvy. Defoe changes her tone; she now understands full well the law of the sexual marketplace. Moll, who first felt and expressed the pull of love's emotions, ironically learns to glow only when gold glitters.

Though Watt maintains that Defoe writes largely without a developed sense of irony, he must mean the kind of exquisite or sustained tonal irony characteristic of Jane Austen or Henry James. There are other kinds of irony present in Defoe; indeed, the irony toward which he is drawn helps place the action of the novel in the context of those contingencies that make up a texture for realism or psychological realism.

In Defoe's fiction characters tend to form opinions about actions before those actions have time to develop, or they act before the implications of their actions are clear. The gap between speech and action, between impulse and resolution, is the ironic dimension in which Defoe works. Irony is directed against Defoe's characters as the price paid for impulsive thinking. And his characters learn in the course of their lives how great a price is exacted from them. Again, an instance of what I mean occurs in *Moll Flanders* when Moll, inured to a life of theft, steals a horse on the street, though there is nothing she can do with it and no place to put it. Taking the horse becomes an ironic commentary on impulse; she does not steal merely for the sake of necessity but for the thrill, and the thrill departs soon enough when she stands in the middle of the street all forlorn with horse in hand.

What Defoe does in scenes such as these is create destabilizing moments within a fiction that end up two-timing his characters. Irony separates impulse from necessity and only after a lag time does recognition catch up to action. Such ironies can even extend over several years, as is the case when Crusoe builds a canoe out of a log without the least idea of how to bring the craft to water: "I could no more turn her, and set her upright upon her bottom, than I could remove the Island" (125). He tries to draw moral lessons from the incident, leaving the hulk inland as an emblem of his folly, but the inherent, almost Chaplinesque, irony of the scene takes precedence.

On other occasions Crusoe can ramble on about a subject until a single contingent event turns him around in place, say, the scene in which he exults about providential corn—"God had miraculously caus'd this Grain to grow without any Help of Seed sown" (78)—but then realizes he spilled the seeds himself: "at last it occur'd to my Thoughts, that I had shook a Bag of Chickens Meat out in that Place, and then the Wonder began to cease" (78). The almost passive naturalism of "the Wonder began to cease" is the measure of Defoe's ironic entrance into Crusoe's mercurial mind, which then shortens the distance between exultation and realization: "I must confess, my religious Thankfulness to God's Providence began to abate too upon the Discovering that all this was nothing but what was common" (78). On the other hand, providence assured "that 10 or 12 Grains of Corn should remain unspoil'd" (79). All this is wry, whatever larger philosophical implications readers wish to glean from it.

Crusoe often seeks certainty in expression or in execution, but he experiences doubt and anxiety. The inevitable result is bafflement. Defoe is excellent at recording it. When Crusoe tries to explain the nature of evil to Friday he ties himself in casuistical knots. *"Why God no kill the Devil, so make him no more do wicked?"* (218), Friday asks. Crusoe sputters a bit and then tries the oldest dodge in the world: "I was strangely surpiz'd at his Question, and after all, tho' I was now an old Man, yet I was but a young Doctor, and ill enough qualified for a Casuist, or a Solver of Difficulties: And at first I could not tell what to say, so I pretended not to hear him, and ask'd him what he said?" (218). Crusoe is, at best, only minimally aware of the irony here; even if he asks for a repeat of the question he is no better suited to answer it.

A slightly different aspect of Defoe's irony has annoyed some of his critics, baffled others, and amused a few—his ironic wit. Wit for Defoe resides in the energies of his language and touches on the same goal as the detail of his circumstantial description. What he tries to do with wit is represent the way language reflects the habits, inconsistencies, anxieties, and self-deprecating waverings of his characters. Defoe accomplishes surprising things with language in this regard, allowing his characters to turn clichés just that notch that reenlivens them, to overstate or understate an experience in ways appropriate to their reaction to it, to develop or extenuate a joke that begins in subtlety and ends in broadness.

Some of the same effects prevail in Defoe's journalism and poetry, where even his titles mimic clichés. Take, for example, *The True-Born Englishman* (1701), possibly the most popular poem of its day. The poem is an attack against xenophobia or excessive national pride, and its clichéd title puffs up the object of derision. There is haughtiness in it; there is a sense that one can be true born, that it means something to be so, and that anyone with sense can recognize the quality, the distinction, the superiority implied. Yet the title stands in ironic opposition to the drift of the poem's argument. Defoe's first impulse is always to bring the image forth, to inflate its language or render the image ironic before he deflates it.

Early in the island adventure, for example, Crusoe prepares to bed down for the night. The sequence of activity is at once natural and inherently funny. Crusoe wanders inland for a drink of fresh water, places a small bit of tobacco in his mouth to stave his hunger, sights a bush fir tree, "and having cut me a short Stick, like a Truncheon, for my Defence, I took up my Lodging" (47). Whereas the truncheon for defense makes perfect sense, "took up my Lodging" is a traveler's cliché charged by bizarre circumstance. Crusoe knows the phrase is commonplace and inappropriate, but, in another sense, it works psychologically to normalize his situation, to give him a sense of security.

There are abundant instances throughout the adventure of Defoe writing in this manner. Crusoe is terrified during a cave-in while enlarging his mountain hollow. In his journal he has calmed down enough to record the incident as if the economy of his wit sufficed for his possible demise: "for if I had been under it I had never wanted a Grave-Digger" (74). When Crusoe figures out after a long and frustrating process of trial and error how to make bread from his corn supply he concludes, "It might be truly said, that now I work'd for my Bread" (118). It is not simply that Crusoe thinks the sentiment accurate and applicable, but he likes the playful turn on the expression. He gets a certain linguistic pleasure out of making the symbolic literal. Now that he is at ease language works for him; his sense of the joke in the cliché serves as a kind of belated release from the very real work he did for his very real loaf of bread.

Defoe encourages a smile from his reader by allowing a smile in his hero. Crusoe thinks of the power he holds on his island, and it is not enough for him to survey his domain; he amuses himself by parodying absolute tyranny: "I had the lives of all my Subjects at my absolute Command. I could hang, draw, give Liberty, and take it away, and no Rebels among all my Subjects" (148). Of course, he has no subjects. Moreover, he knows how he would have looked to the more normal of his former countrymen: "But had any one in *England* been to meet such a Man as I was, it must either have frighted them, or rais'd a great deal of Laughter" (149). He then goes into a famous description of his appearance that amuses him no end. He is what he can piece together, and he has as little respect for his tailoring ability as he had earlier for his carpentry: "for if I was a bad *Carpenter,* I was a worse *Taylor*" (135). "I had a short Jacket of Goat-Skin, the Skirts coming down to about the middle of my Thighs; and a Pair of open-knee'd Breeches of the same, the Breeches were made of the Skin of an old *He-goat,* whose Hair hung down such a Length on either Side, that like *Pantaloons* it reach'd to the middle of my Legs" (149).

To imagine Crusoe chasing his own goats around the large preserve he had made for them in this garb is to imagine a scene out of old Greek comedy (and perhaps to answer the recessed question of Crusoe's sex life on the island). But Defoe only has Crusoe top off his riotous self-portrait by a reference to his long whiskers that plays on an idiom as familiar to eighteenth-century ears as to twentieth-century ones: "I will not say they were long enough to hang my Hat upon them; but they were of a Length and Shape monstrous enough, and such as in *England* would have pass'd for frightful" (150). This comes to roost later when Crusoe claims authority over the motley collection of natives, captives, and mutineers washed up on his island, but cannot bear to appear in front of them with his ridiculous skins and monstrous mustaches. Crusoe's language is wittily self aware: "I retir'd in the Dark from them, that they might not see what Kind of a Governour they had" (269).

During the *Tempest*-like shenanigans on the island at the end of the narrative the self-deprecating games Crusoe plays with the nomenclature of sovereignty and power become fairly elaborate. He is at the crossroads of two jokes: first, the mock power he has held over his island, and second, the absurdity of his looks. When he pretends to the role of supreme governor he cannot do so in those

Crusoe's whiskers, "long enough to hang [his] hat upon them."
Engraving by Grandville, from Robinson Crusoe *(New York: D. Appleton & Co., 1901).*

frightful goatskins. So he passes himself off, like the future ragtag man of Conrad's *Heart of Darkness,* as an envoy who does the governor's dirty work: "so I now appear'd as another Person, and spoke of the Governour, the Garrison, the Castle, and the like, upon all Occasions" (271). Crusoe is having good fun with all this, and his exuberance in thinking about himself and the way he looks adds more to the realism of Defoe's style than the situation itself. By this time in the narrative, the action is beginning to resemble a Marx Brothers movie.

Other elements of expression in Defoe's writing characterize his style and afford thematic access into the action of *Robinson Crusoe.* Crusoe is a man alone in a physical space, and his story is in many ways about the naming of things in order to control or possess them. His first entry in his journal hints at this. Crusoe calls the place *"the Island of Despair"* (70), but that is far from the last of the things he calls his island. Names for Crusoe become actual conditions that change in relation to psychological circumstance, and his situation on his island is readable according to his state of mind. What he calls the island is his way of allegorizing it, accruing meaning from names, so that Despair, if Crusoe manages to get back to his island after running adrift from it in a canoe, can become Deliverance. If he is confident, his preserve becomes his Settlement; if he is frightened, it becomes his Fortress.

In fact, how Crusoe names island spaces constitutes a good measure of his activity. The primary psychological facet of the adventure is Crusoe's conversion of his island terrain from disaster to homestead. He must make a forbidding and strange place a habitual place, a resubstantiated home. In a larger sense, perhaps touching on the allegorical dimension of the story to which Defoe himself referred, all life is about the process of making the alien familiar. Defoe's naming of things tips off the process. Crusoe's island vocabulary reveals the way he converts things in his own mind, the way he names his securities and his fears. Defoe allows him to build psychological ports of call in his mind, just as when he first seeks a small creek or river inlet for the goods he takes by raft from the shipwreck that "I might make use of as a Port to get to Land with my Cargo" (51). This sentence makes of Crusoe's new life a version of his old; the scale is reduced but the process is the same as for any merchant adventurer.

Similarly, Crusoe as self-regulator and governor of his island does not simply decide things; rather, he presides as in participatory democracy: "then I call'd a Council, that is to say, in my Thoughts, whether I should take back the Raft, but this appear'd impracticable" (54). Crusoe is always using conversational waystations—"that is to say" or "as I might say" or "as I called it to my self"—to mark those moments in which he knows that his phrasing is part of his island psychology in domesticating and controlling his spaces. Here are some typical examples. He extends his space outside his rock by putting up a ramshackle series of posts with ship's cable, and when the object takes shape it gets a new name: "I have already describ'd my Habitation, which was a Tent under the Side of a Rock, surrounded with a strong Pale of Posts and Cables, but I might now rather call it a Wall" (67). When he digs through the rock and feels even safer he changes the nomenclature again: "my Pale or Fortification" (67).

His island soon represents in miniature a version of the world for Crusoe. He can be castaway on the island and at home at the same time, as when he walks inland and spends the night apart from his original habitation, "the first Night, as I might say, I had lain from home" (99). Crusoe's language reveals the same compelling lure of settlement his father had recommended years earlier in terms of remaining on the home island of England. After a long journey by foot around his island, or as much as he could negotiate, Crusoe sounds like the most weary and timid of voyagers: "my own House, as I call'd it to my self, was a perfect Settlement to me, compar'd to that" (111). Only by a process of familiarization can that settlement be a perfect one for him. On another *periplou* or island voyage, this one by canoe, Crusoe has drifted so far from his point of embarkation that he refers to catching a lucky eddy back to the island as a "Reprieve." He gets all confused in his language about what exactly represents what. Is he delivered home to the island upon which, as castaway, he is marooned? "When I was on Shore I fell on my Knees and gave God Thanks for my Deliverance, resolving to lay aside all Thought of my Deliverance by my Boat, and refreshing my self with such Things as I had, I brought my Boat close to the Shore in a little Cove that I had spy'd under some Trees, and lay'd me down to sleep, being quite spent with the Labour and Fatigue of the Voyage" (141).

In this instance Crusoe is not even aware of the double positioning his new home entails, but in others he knows precisely what his language does for him, as when he refers to his castaway condition as both opportunity and punishment, "my Reign, or my Captivity, which you please" (173). The "which you please" is an insight. Crusoe invites the reader of his account to participate in the process of conversion he undergoes. The same is true when Crusoe describes the arrival of Friday on his island. His language turns the scene toward his own psychological perspective. Given all that a reader comes to know about the way Crusoe marks space on his island and adjusts the notion of possession to self-expression, it is fitting that when he views Friday escaping his cannibal captors late in the narrative he notices that the man "ran with incredible Swiftness along the Sands directly toward me, I mean towards that part of the Coast, where my Habitation was" (201). This is a slip that is not a slip. It even occurs to Crusoe that the native is meant for him, though he quickly qualifies a possessive locution with a spatial one. To have learned anything about how to read the narrative is to have learned that possession is spatial in the world of Crusoe. Toward me and toward my habitation mean the same thing. Crusoe corrects his phrasing only because the reader might think that Crusoe is part of the escaping native's consciousness whereas the escaping native is really part of his.

Defoe's style here reflects, ironically in one sense and accurately in another, one of the lessons of fictional realism. Every detail of locution counts, everything is readable. But at the same time everything had better be readable in terms of the particular exigencies of its placement in the story. Symbolic interpretation of any kind is fine and well, but it should take place in proper sequence, only after the realistic texture of the narrative is set carefully, painstakingly in place. This is what makes the novel as a genre distinctive, and this is what makes Defoe's role in inaugurating the novel with *Robinson Crusoe* in 1719 so significant.

Notes and References

1. Samuel Coleridge wrote marginalia in his own edition of *Crusoe*. See *Marginalia*, vol. 2, ed. George Whalley (Princeton: Princeton University Press, 1984), 167; hereafter cited in the text.

2. James Joyce, *Ulysses*, the corrected text, ed. Hans Walter Gabler (New York: Random House, 1986), 90; hereafter cited in the text.

3. Joyce's remarks are from a lecture on Defoe in 1912 delivered in Italian in Trieste. The lecture is translated in "Daniel Defoe," *Buffalo Studies* 1 (1964): 14; hereafter cited in the text.

4. The relation of Defoe's novels to the religious traditions they imitated is treated fully by Paul Hunter, *The Reluctant Pilgrim* (Baltimore: Johns Hopkins University Press, 1966), and by George Starr, *Defoe and Spiritual Biography* (Princeton University Press, 1971).

5. Charles Gildon, *The Life and Strange Surprizing Adventures of Mr. D----- De F-- of London, Hosier* (London, 1719), ix–x; hereafter cited in the text.

6. James Boswell, *Life of Johnson*, vol. 1, ed. G. B. Hill (Oxford: Clarendon Press, 1887), 322.

7. Jonathan Swift, *Examiner*, 16 November 1710, no. 15, in *Works*, vol. 3, ed. Herbert Davis (Oxford: Basil Blackwell, 1941), 13.

8. Jonathan Swift, *Gulliver's Travels*, in *Works*, 11: 283.

9. Most recently F. Bastian in *Defoe's Early Life* (Totowa, N. J.: Barnes & Noble, 1981), makes the fullest case for the immersion of Defoe into his fictional subjects, though caution is well advised for some of Bastian's highly speculative readings.

10. James Sutherland, *Defoe* (London: Methuen, 1937), 228; hereafter cited in the text.

11. *The Letters of Daniel Defoe*, ed. G. H. Healy (Oxford: Clarendon Press, 1955), 158.

12. Marcel Proust, *The Remembrance of Things Past*, vol. 3, trans. C. K. Scott Moncrieff, Terence Kilmartin, and Andreas Mayor (New York: Random House, 1981), 459.

13. *The Odyssey*, trans. Robert Fitzgerald (New York: Doubleday Anchor Books, 1961), book 24, p. 454; hereafter cited in the text.

14. *Defoe's Review*, 11 June 1713, facsimile edition, vol. 9, ed. Arthur Wellesley Secord (New York: Columbia University Press, 1938), 214; hereafter cited in the text.

15. Maximillian Novak concludes rightly of later plans for the island that "Crusoe's island colony must have been the product of one of Defoe's oldest daydreams" (*Realism, Myth, and History in Defoe's Fiction* [Lincoln: University of Nebraska Press, 1983], 27).

16. Simon Schama, *The Embarrassment of Riches: An Interpretation of Dutch Culture in the Golden Age* (New York: Alfred A. Knopf, 1987), 29; hereafter cited in the text.

17. Jean-Jacques Rousseau, *The Confessions*, trans. J. M. Cohen (Harmondsworth, England: Penguin, 1953), 550.

18. James Joyce, *Finnegans Wake* (New York: Viking, 1939), 184.

19. See Robert W. Ayers, "*Robinson Crusoe*: 'Allusive Allegorick History,' " *PMLA* 82 (1967): 399–407, for a rundown on the meaning of Crusoe's name.

20. See Maximillian Novak, *Economics and the Fiction of Daniel Defoe* (Berkeley: University of California Press, 1962), especially his chapter "Robinson Crusoe's Original Sin," 32–48.

21. See Christopher Flint, "Orphaning the Family: The Role of Kinship in *Robinson Crusoe*," *English Literary History* 55 (1988): 381–419; and Richard Braverman, "Crusoe's Legacy," *Studies in the Novel* 18 (1986): 1–26.

22. For the best survey of why or why not *Robinson Crusoe* serves as an economic fable, see Novak, *Economics and the Fiction of Daniel Defoe*, 49–66.

23. Karl Marx, *Capital: A Critique of Political Economy*, vol. 1, trans. Ben Fowkes (Harmondsworth, England: Penguin, 1987), 171.

24. J. M. Coetzee, *Foe* (New York: Viking Penguin, 1987), 23.

Bibliography

Primary Works

The Life and Surprizing Adventures of Robinson Crusoe, of York, Mariner. Edited by J. Donald Crowley. Oxford English Novels series. London: Oxford University Press, 1972.
The Works of Daniel Defoe. Edited by G. A. Maynadier. 16 vols. New York: Sproul, 1903–4.
Defoe's Review. Edited by Arthur Wellesley Secord. 9 vols. New York: Columbia University Press, 1938.
Robinson Crusoe: An Authoritative Text, Backgrounds and Sources, Criticism. Edited by Michael Shinagel. New York: W. W. Norton, 1975.

Secondary Works

Bibliographies

Hutchins, Henry L. *Robinson Crusoe and Its Printing, 1719–1731.* New York: Columbia University Press, 1925.
Moore, John Robert. *A Checklist of the Writings of Daniel Defoe.* Bloomington: Indiana University Press, 1960.
Novak, Maximillian. "Daniel Defoe." In *The New Cambridge Bibliography of English Literature,* edited by G. Watson, vol. 2, 706–7. Cambridge: Cambridge University Press, 1971.

Biography and Background

Backscheider, Paula. *Daniel Defoe: His Life.* Baltimore: Johns Hopkins University Press, 1989.

Bastian, F. *Defoe's Early Life*. Totowa, N. J.: Barnes & Noble Books, 1981.

Byrd, Max, ed. *Daniel Defoe: A Collection of Critical Essays*. Englewood Cliffs, N. J.: Prentice-Hall, 1976.

Chalmers, George. *The Life of Defoe*. London: Stockdale, 1790.

Earle, Peter. *The World of Defoe*. New York: Atheneum, 1977.

Ellis, Frank H., ed. *Twentieth Century Interpretations of Robinson Crusoe: A Collection of Critical Essays*. Englewood Cliffs, N. J.: Prentice-Hall, 1969.

Healey, G. H. *The Letters of Daniel Defoe*. Oxford: Oxford University Press, 1955.

Heidenreich, H. *The Libraries of Daniel Defoe and Phillips Farewell*. Berlin, 1970. A useful sales catalogue of Defoe's personal library.

Lee, William. *Daniel Defoe: His Life and Recently Discovered Writings*. London: J. C. Hotten, 1869.

Moore, John Robert. *Daniel Defoe, Citizen of the Modern World*. Chicago: University of Chicago Press, 1958.

Rogers, Pat, ed. *Defoe: The Critical Heritage*. London: Routledge & Kegan Paul, 1972.

Sutherland, James. *Defoe*. London: Methuen, 1937.

Trent, William. *Defoe: How to Know Him*. Indianapolis: Bobbs-Merrill, 1916.

Wright, Thomas. *The Life of Daniel Defoe*. London: Farncombe, 1931.

Books on Defoe's Fiction

Alkon, Paul. *Defoe and Fictional Time*. Athens: University of Georgia Press, 1979. An important study of the way time controls the disposition of Defoe's fiction.

Blewett, David. *Defoe's Art of Fiction*. Toronto: University of Toronto Press, 1979. A study of the design and craft of Defoe's work as a novelist.

Boardman, Michael. *Defoe and the Uses of Narrative*. Toronto: University of Toronto Press, 1979. An intelligent look at the various narrative strategies in Defoe's fiction and their purposes.

Coetzee, J. *Foe*. New York: Viking Penguin, 1987. A revisionary version of the action on Crusoe's island, adding a woman character.

Gildon, Charles. *The Life and Strange Surprizing Adventures of Mr. D - - - - - De F - -, of London, Hosier*. London, 1719. The first critical reaction to *Crusoe*, an intriguing one in that it reveals the way Defoe's contemporaries, especially hostile ones, viewed his fiction.

Hunter, Paul. *The Reluctant Pilgrim*. Baltimore: Johns Hopkins Press, 1966. A landmark study of Defoe's fiction in relation to archetypical narratives of religious quests, crises, and conversions.

Bibliography

Novak, Maximillian. *Defoe and the Nature of Man*. London: Oxford University Press, 1963. Places Defoe's fiction in the context of natural law and natural rights theory in the seventeenth and eighteenth centuries.
———. *Economics and the Fiction of Daniel Defoe*. Berkeley: University of California Press, 1962. A study of the economic bases of Defoe's fiction.
———. *Realism, Myth, and History in Defoe's Fiction*. Lincoln: University of Nebraska Press, 1983. A collection of Novak's important essays, including a crucial one on mythmaking in *Crusoe*.
Richetti, John. *Defoe's Narratives*. London: Oxford University Press, 1975. One of the best critical treatments of Defoe's novels, centering on how the novelistic imagination embodies literary and historical issues.
Rogers, Pat. *Robinson Crusoe*. London: Allen & Unwin, 1979. A fine casebook or overview of the novel with useful appendixes on travel literature germane to *Crusoe*.
Secord, Arthur Wellesley. *Studies in the Narrative Method of Defoe*. Urbana: University of Illinois Press, 1916. An early work on Defoe's transformation of source material into fiction.
Shinagel, Michael. *Defoe and Middle-Class Gentility*. Cambridge, Mass.: Harvard University Press, 1968. An excellent study on the role of social class in the evolution of fiction.
Sill, Geoffrey M. *Defoe and the Idea of Fiction, 1713–1719*. Newark: University of Delaware Press, 1983. A study of the immediate background to the writing of Defoe's major novels.
Starr, G. A. *Defoe and Casuistry*. Princeton: Princeton University Press, 1971. An important study on the way Defoe argues issues in his fiction, and the relation of those arguments to contemporary controversies and debates.
———. *Defoe and Spiritual Biography*. Princeton: Princeton University Press, 1965. A landmark study on Defoe's use of spiritual biography as a model for his fiction.
Sutherland, James. *Daniel Defoe: A Critical Study*. Cambridge, Mass.: Harvard University Press, 1971. A general study of Defoe's work remarkable for its good sense and its powerful writing.
Tournier, Michel. *Friday*. Translated by Norman Denny. New York: Pantheon Books, 1985. A revisionary novel of Crusoe's island life, with the emphasis shifted to Friday.
Zimmerman, Everett. *Defoe and the Novel*. Berkeley and Los Angeles: University of California Press, 1975. An excellent study of the way Defoe adapts matters of intellectual importance to his time into the design of his fiction.

Chapters on *Robinson Crusoe* in Books on English Fiction

Adams, Percy. *Travel Literature and the Evolution of the Novel.* Lexington: University of Kentucky Press, 1983. A full background account of the travel literature in which Defoe displayed an interest.

Baker, E. A. *The History of the English Novel.* 10 vols. London: Witherby, 1924–39. Volume 3 includes an excellent essay on the evolution of *Crusoe* as a novel.

Bender, John. *Imagining the Penitentiary: Fiction and the Architecture of Mind in Eighteenth-Century England.* Chicago: University of Chicago Press, 1987. An intriguing new study about the spatial forms of the imagination that includes fine work on *Crusoe.*

Brooks, Douglas. *Number and Pattern in the Eighteenth-Century Novel.* London: Routledge & Kegan Paul, 1973. Treats the allegorical potential of the timing of Crusoe's island stay.

Carnochan, W. B. *Confinement and Flight: An Essay on English Literature of the Eighteenth Century.* Berkeley: University of California Press, 1977. Contains an excellent psychological study of Crusoe on his island.

Damrosch, Leopold. *God's Plot and Man's Stories.* Chicago: University of Chicago Press, 1985. The *Crusoe* chapter is the latest on the novel's religious plotting.

Gove, P. B. *The Imaginary Voyage in Prose Fiction.* New York: Columbia University Press, 1941. A landmark study on the imaginative voyage, with useful material on *Crusoe.*

McKeon, Michael. *Origins of the English Novel, 1600–1740.* Baltimore: Johns Hopkins University Press, 1987. The *Crusoe* chapter deals with the adaptation of older narrative forms to the new circumstances of secular fiction in the age.

McKillop, Alan D. *The Early Masters of English Fiction.* Lawrence, Kans.: University of Kansas Press, 1975. The *Crusoe* chapter is still one of the best and most insightful readings available.

Tillyard, E. M. *The Epic Strain in the English Novel.* London: Chatto and Windus, 1958. The *Crusoe* chapter deals with the newer narrative forms in which epic themes and structures appear in the eighteenth century.

Watt, Ian. *The Rise of the Novel.* Berkeley: University of California Press, 1957. Contains a landmark essay on Crusoe as a mythic embodiment of Western culture.

Woolf, Virginia. *The Second Common Reader.* New York: Harcourt Brace, 1925. Contains a fine piece on Defoe's fictional style.

Bibliography

Journal Articles on *Robinson Crusoe*

Ayers, Robert W. "Robinson Crusoe: 'Allusive Allegorick History.' " *PMLA* 82 (1967): 399–407. A ranging essay on Defoe's sense of allegory and narrative.

Berne, E. "The Psychological Structure of Space with Some Remarks on *Robinson Crusoe.*" *Psychoanalytic Quarterly* 25 (1956): 549–57. The first thoroughgoing Freudian reading of Crusoe's phobias.

Braudy, Leo. "Daniel Defoe and the Anxieties of Autobiography." *Genre* 6 (1973): 76–90. An intriguing essay that treats the instabilities of autobiographical narrative.

Braverman, Richard. "Crusoe's Legacy." *Studies in the Novel* 18 (1986): 1–26. A brilliant short study of the political economics of Crusoe's story.

Brown, Homer O. "The Displaced Self in the Novels of Daniel Defoe." *English Literary History* 38 (1971): 562–90. A clever reading of Crusoe, and other of Defoe's characters, as self-projectors.

Fishman, Burton J. "Defoe, Herman Moll and the Geography of South America." *Huntington Library Quarterly* 36 (1973): 227–38. Focuses on the region where Crusoe is marooned.

Flint, Christopher. "Orphaning the Family: The Role of Kinship in *Robinson Crusoe.*" *English Literary History* 55 (1988): 381–419. The best essay on the web of human relations, insofar as that web exists, in the *Crusoe* saga.

Joyce, James. "Daniel Defoe." Translated from Italian by Joseph Prescott. *Buffalo Studies* 1 (1964): 3–25. A lecture Joyce delivered in Italian as a companion to one on William Blake. It contains wonderful observations on the nature of Defoe's material imagination.

Novak, Maximillian. "Crusoe the King and the Political Evolution of His Island." *Studies in English Literature* 2 (1962): 337–50. A crucial essay on the nature of sovereignty in *Crusoe.*

———. "Defoe's Theory of Fiction." *Studies in Philology* 61 (1964): 650–68. A review of the issues that formed and framed Defoe's idea of the practice of fiction.

Parker, G. "The Allegory of *Robinson Crusoe.*" *Review of English Studies* 10 (1925): 11–25. An essay that first suggested the nature of the personal allegory in *Crusoe.*

Seidel, Michael. "Crusoe in Exile." *PMLA* 96 (1981): 363–74. Explores the literary and political nature of displacement in *Crusoe.*

Watt, Ian. "*Robinson Crusoe* as a Myth." *Essays in Criticism,* 1 (1951): 95–119. The original version of the famous essay reconceived for Watt's *The Rise of the Novel.*

Index

Index

The Author

Michael Seidel is professor of English and comparative literature at Columbia University, where he has taught for the last twelve years. He has written on a variety of literary subjects and topics from the eighteenth to the twentieth centuries. His books include a study of James Joyce and the epic tradition, *Epic Geography: James Joyce's Ulysses* (1976); an account of the history of narrative satire, *Satiric Inheritance: Rabelais to Sterne* (1979); and a meditation on the pattern of exile in prose fiction, *Exile and the Narrative Imagination* (1986). He is an advisory editor for *James Joyce Studies* and a volume editor for a California-based multivolume edition of *The Works of Daniel Defoe*. Under a different dispensation, and wearing something other than a scholarly hat, he has chronicled Joe DiMaggio's great hitting streak of 1941, *Joe DiMaggio and the Summer of '41* (1988); written a speculative essay on baseball and television, "Field and Screen," in *Meaning of the Medium* (1990); and has just completed a biography of Red Sox star Ted Williams.